Culinary Arts Institute

The DESSERT Book

Featured in cover photo:
a. Mandarin-Glazed Cheese Cake, 76
b. Frozen Chocolate Mousse, 43
c. Berries and Cream, 30

The DESSERT Book

THE DESSERT BOOK

The Culinary Arts Institute Staff:

Helen Geist: Director
Sherrill Weary: Editor • Helen Lehman: Assistant Editor
Edward Finnegan: Executive Editor • Charles Bozett: Art Director
Ethel La Roche: Editorial Assistant • Ivanka Simatic: Recipe Tester
Malinda Miller: Copy Editor • John Mahalek: Art Assembly

Book designed and coordinated by Charles Bozett and Laurel DiGangi

Illustrations by Kay Smith

Cover photo: Zdenek Pivecka

Culinary Arts Institute

1975 Hawthorne, Melrose Park, Illinois, 60160

PHOTO ACKNOWLEDGMENTS
American Dairy Association; C and H Sugar Kitchen
Diamond Walnut Growers, Inc.; Jell-o Gelatin
Sterno, Inc.; Sunkist, Inc.
United Fresh Fruit and Vegetable Association

Introduction

Surely everyone has at one time had a craving for a piece of angel food cake like grandmother used to make. Or on a hot August night longed for some cool and creamy vanilla ice cream just churned in the ice cream freezer. Modern-day versions of these and other favorites (including brownies, shortcake, fudge, and Boston Cream Pie) have been included in *The Dessert Book* along with lots of new and elegant desserts.

Since prepared desserts are so readily available, one would think home baking isn't as popular as it used to be. With the recipes we have included here, homemade dessert can be as easy as 1-2-3! Some desserts will take a bit more time and patience, but the enthusiastic compliments received will make the effort worthwhile. When choosing a dessert, consider the rest of the meal. If dinner is heavy, hearty, or spicy, choose fresh fruit or a cooling sherbet. For a pleasant finish to a light meal, a dessert such as fruit pie, frosted cake, or rich pastry is well received. Dinner and dessert are partners, so let them complement each other.

Don't wait for a special occasion to make a new dessert. Try it out on your family and guests soon. Children especially look forward to dessert and are often told, "When you finish your dinner, dessert will be served." Puddings, custards, and cobblers often satisfy the dessert desires of most family members. Commercial ice cream topped with a warm homemade sauce is sometimes just what makes dinner complete.

For the perfect ending to dinner-time entertaining, prepare a dessert that makes an impression by its appearance alone.

Guests will marvel at a towering soufflé or flaming Cherries Jubilee, or wonder how you ever made such a flaky strudel.

When people begin to count calories, desserts are usually the first item placed on the "no, no" list. But desserts don't have to be made with butter, whipping cream, and sugar to be good. With that in mind, low-calorie desserts are included in a special section of this book.

Desserts don't have to wait for dinner to make an appearance. Dessert parties are a great way to welcome new neighbors, refresh the bridge club, satisfy a gathering of den mothers; or they can just be an excuse for friends to get together. *The Dessert Book* is full of recipes that can be made ahead and presented with ease, leaving little work for the hostess at serving time.

For summertime fun, have an ice cream social. There are enough ice creams, sherbets, and ices in the frozen dessert section to tempt everyone! Serve with an assortment of cakes, cookies, and toppings for the perfect party on a lazy Sunday afternoon.

Going on a picnic? Don't forget to take dessert. Anything that requires refrigeration is best left at home, but lots of desserts are available from which to choose. Easy to pack, carry, and serve, cupcakes, cookies, and many cakes make excellent travelers.

The CULINARY ARTS INSTITUTE is pleased to share with you this assortment of dessert recipes. No matter what the occasion, weather, or time of year, we're sure you'll find a dessert you'll want to serve. Everyone loves dessert, so "let them eat cake," or pudding, or pie, as long as they're all homemade!

Contents

Custards, Puddings, and Soufflés

Pots de Crème Chocolat

2 cups whipping cream
1 tablespoon sugar
4 ounces sweet chocolate, melted
6 egg yolks, beaten
1½ teaspoons vanilla extract

1. Heat the cream and sugar together in the top of a double boiler over simmering water until cream is scalded. Add the melted chocolate and stir until blended. Pour mixture into beaten egg yolks, beating constantly until blended. Stir in vanilla extract.
2. Strain through a fine sieve into 8 small earthenware pots or custard cups. Set pots in a pan of hot water.
3. Bake at 325°F 20 minutes. (Mixture will become thicker upon cooling.)
4. Set cups on wire rack to cool; chill thoroughly.

8 servings

Crème Brûlée

4 egg yolks, slightly beaten
¼ cup sugar
2 cups whipping cream, scalded
2 teaspoons vanilla extract
½ cup firmly packed brown sugar

1. Combine egg yolks with sugar; blend thoroughly. Gradually add hot cream, stirring until sugar is dissolved. Strain into a 1-quart baking dish.
2. Blend in vanilla extract. Place baking dish in a shallow pan with hot water and bake at 325°F 50 minutes, or until a knife inserted in custard comes out clean.
3. Remove from oven and set baking dish on wire rack to cool; chill thoroughly.
4. Before serving, sift brown sugar evenly over top. Place under broiler with top at least 5 inches from heat; broil until sugar is melted. Watch carefully so sugar will not burn.
5. Cool and refrigerate until ready to serve.

About 6 servings

Trifle

Pound cake
½ cup brandy or rum
¼ cup sugar
1 envelope unflavored gelatin
⅛ teaspoon salt
5 egg yolks
1¾ cups milk
1 teaspoon vanilla extract
3 egg whites
¼ cup sugar
¼ cup chilled whipping cream, whipped

1. Cut pound cake into 1-inch pieces. Arrange in a layer over bottom of a 2-quart shallow casserole. Pour brandy over cake pieces. Set aside.
2. Combine ¼ cup sugar, gelatin, and salt in the top of a double boiler; blend thoroughly. Beat egg yolks with milk in a bowl until thoroughly blended. Combine with the gelatin mixture in top of double boiler.
3. Set over boiling water and cook, stirring occasionally, about 5 minutes, or until the gelatin is completely dissolved. Remove from heat and stir in vanilla extract. Chill until mixture mounds slightly when dropped from a spoon; stir occasionally.
4. Beat the egg whites until frothy. Add ¼ cup sugar gradually, beating thoroughly after each addition. Continue to beat until stiff peaks are formed.
5. Spread egg whites and whipped cream over gelatin mixture and gently fold together. Turn into casserole. Chill until firm.
6. When ready to serve, garnish with **candied cherries, slivered almonds,** and **pieces of angelica.** If desired, garnish with a border of sweetened whipped cream forced through a pastry bag and star decorating tube.

About 12 servings

Chafing Dish Oeufs à la Neige

Meringues:
3 egg whites (at room temperature)
⅛ teaspoon salt
6 tablespoons sugar
¼ teaspoon vanilla extract

Custard:
6 egg yolks
¼ cup sugar
⅛ teaspoon salt
2½ cups milk
1½ teaspoons vanilla extract
Grated orange peel
Strawberries, sliced

1. Pour hot water to a depth of 2 inches in water pan of chafing dish. Heat to simmering.
2. To make meringues, beat egg whites and salt in a small bowl until frothy. Gradually beat in sugar, 1 tablespoon at a time. Continue to beat until stiff peaks form, beating in vanilla extract with last few strokes.
3. Drop meringue by heaping tablespoonfuls onto simmering water, poaching 6 at a time. Cover, and poach meringues 3 to 5 minutes, or until puffed and slightly dry to the touch. Remove from water using a slotted spoon and place in blazer pan.
4. Remove some of the poaching water so blazer pan will not touch water when set in place. Keep water warm.
5. To make custard, beat egg yolks in a heavy 2-quart saucepan. Stir in sugar and salt. Gradually stir in milk. Place over low heat and cook until custard coats a metal spoon, stirring constantly. Stir in vanilla extract.
6. Pour custard around meringues in blazer pan, allowing meringues to float. Sprinkle orange peel over meringues and garnish with strawberries.
7. Place blazer pan over warm water. Serve dessert warm; do not overheat or custard will curdle.

6 servings

Meringue Shells

6 egg whites
¼ teaspoon salt
¾ teaspoon cream of tartar
1½ cups sugar
Custard Filling
Cherry-Cinnamon Sauce (page 37)

1. Beat egg whites with salt and cream of tartar until frothy. Gradually add sugar, continuing to beat until stiff peaks are formed and sugar is dissolved.
2. Shape meringue shells with a spoon or force through a pastry bag and tube onto a baking sheet lined with unglazed paper.
3. Bake at 250°F 1 hour.
4. Transfer meringues from paper to wire racks to cool.
5. When ready to serve, spoon Custard Filling into meringue shells and top with Cherry-Cinnamon Sauce.

12 meringue shells

Custard Filling

½ cup sugar
2 teaspoons flour
¼ teaspoon salt
2 cups milk
6 egg yolks, beaten
1 teaspoon vanilla extract

1. Blend sugar, flour, and salt in a heavy saucepan. Stir in the milk. Bring to boiling; stir and cook 1 to 2 minutes.
2. Add a small amount of the hot mixture to egg yolks, stirring constantly. Blend into mixture in saucepan. Cook 1 minute.
3. Remove from heat and cool immediately by pouring custard into a chilled bowl and setting it in refrigerator or pan of cold water. Blend vanilla extract into cooled custard. Chill until serving time.

About 2½ cups filling

Meringues au Chocolat: Fill meringue shells with Chocolate-Mocha Cream Pudding (page 13). Garnish with **unsweetened whipped cream** and **coarsely chopped salted nuts.**

Meringues with Blueberries: Fill meringue shells with **fresh blueberries.** Top each with a dollop of **dairy sour cream** and a sprinkling of **brown sugar.**

Soft Custard

¼ cup sugar
⅛ teaspoon salt
3 eggs, slightly beaten
2 cups milk, scalded
2 teaspoons vanilla extract

1. Add sugar and salt to beaten eggs and beat just until blended. Stirring constantly, gradually add scalded milk.
2. Strain mixture into a double-boiler top and cook, stirring constantly, over simmering water until custard coats a metal spoon.
3. Remove from heat and cool to lukewarm over cold water. Stir in vanilla extract. Chill.

4 to 6 servings

Fruit Custard: Follow recipe for Soft Custard. Pour chilled custard over **orange sections, banana slices,** or **well-drained fruit.**

Baked Custard: Follow Soft Custard recipe for mixing ingredients. Strain and blend in vanilla extract. Pour into custard cups and sprinkle each with **nutmeg** (or sprinkle with nutmeg just before serving). Place custard cups in a shallow pan. Set pan with filled cups on oven rack and pour boiling water into pan to a depth of 1 inch. Bake at 325°F 30 to 45 minutes, or until a metal knife inserted halfway between center and edge of custard comes out clean.

Creamy Prune Whip

½ pound dried prunes, cooked and
    pitted
2 tablespoons lemon juice
2 egg whites
⅛ teaspoon salt
½ cup sugar
1 cup chilled whipping cream,
    whipped

1. Force prunes through a food mill or sieve into a bowl. Stir in lemon juice.
2. Beat egg whites with salt until frothy. Add sugar gradually, beating until stiff peaks are formed. Turn beaten egg whites and whipped cream onto prune purée and gently fold together until blended. Chill thoroughly before serving.
3. Spoon into dessert dishes and decorate with swirls of **sweetened whipped cream** and **candied cherries**.

About 6 servings

Celestial Lemon Crème

1 small package lemon pudding and
    pie filling mix
⅓ cup sugar
1½ cups (12-ounce can) pineapple
    juice
    Few grains salt
2 egg yolks
1 cup water
1 cup chilled whipping cream
¼ cup confectioners' sugar
2 cups fresh strawberries, sliced, or
    thawed frozen fruit (strawberry
    halves, raspberries, or sliced
    peaches)
4 ladyfingers, split in halves

1. Combine pudding, ⅓ cup sugar, ¼ cup of the pineapple juice, and salt in a saucepan. Add egg yolks and blend well. Stir in remaining juice and water. Cook and stir until mixture boils and thickens. Remove from heat. Cool thoroughly, stirring frequently.
2. Beat cream until of medium consistency (piles softly); beat in confectioners' sugar with final few strokes. Fold into pudding. Chill at least 1 hour.
3. Spoon one half of the pudding into a serving dish and layer with sliced strawberries (or well-drained fruit). If strawberries are used in a crystal bowl, arrange some slices or halves with the cut side against the glass. Place ladyfinger halves upright around edge of dish, allowing about 1 inch to extend above edge. Cover fruit with remaining pudding. Garnish with whole strawberries or other fruit, if desired.

6 to 8 servings

Coffee Tapioca Parfait

2 egg whites
¼ cup sugar
2 egg yolks, slightly beaten
3 cups milk
⅓ cup sugar
⅓ cup quick-cooking tapioca
2 tablespoons instant coffee
¼ teaspoon salt
1 teaspoon vanilla extract
    Salted pecans or almonds, chopped
    Whipped cream

1. Beat egg whites until frothy; gradually add ¼ cup sugar, beating until stiff peaks are formed.
2. Combine egg yolks with milk in a saucepan. Add ⅓ cup sugar, tapioca, instant coffee, and salt; mix well. Let stand 5 minutes.
3. Cook and stir over medium heat until mixture comes to a full boil; do not overcook.
4. Remove from heat and immediately stir a small amount of the hot mixture into egg white mixture. Then quickly blend in the remaining hot mixture, vanilla extract, and nuts. Cool, stirring once after 15 minutes. Chill.
5. To complete parfait, spoon one third of the tapioca into bottom of chilled parfait glasses; spoon on a layer of whipped cream, sprinkle with **instant coffee,** then **shaved unsweetened chocolate, ground cinnamon,** and **grated orange peel.** Repeat layering two more times, ending with a swirl of whipped cream sprinkled with instant coffee, chocolate, cinnamon, and orange peel.

About 8 servings

Chocolate-Mocha Cream Pudding

2 ounces (2 squares) unsweetened chocolate
1 cup double-strength coffee
⅔ cup sugar
¼ cup flour
¼ teaspoon salt
1 cup milk
3 egg yolks, slightly beaten
2 tablespoons butter or margarine
2 teaspoons vanilla extract

1. Heat chocolate and coffee together over low heat until chocolate is melted; stir to blend.
2. Meanwhile, combine the sugar, flour, and salt in top of a double boiler. Blend in milk.
3. Add the hot coffee-chocolate mixture gradually, stirring until blended. Continue to stir and bring rapidly to boiling; boil 2 minutes.
4. Stir a small amount of hot mixture into the egg yolks. Immediately blend into mixture in double boiler. Cook over simmering water 5 minutes; stir to keep it cooking evenly.
5. Remove from simmering water and blend in butter and vanilla extract. Chill thoroughly before serving or spooning into Meringue Shells (page 11) as a filling.

4 to 6 servings

Rich Chocolate Pudding

2 ounces (2 squares) unsweetened chocolate
2 cups milk
½ cup sugar
2 tablespoons cornstarch
¼ teaspoon salt
2 teaspoons vanilla extract
2 teaspoons butter or margarine

1. Put chocolate and milk into the top of a double boiler. Cook over simmering water until chocolate is melted, stirring occasionally.
2. Combine sugar, cornstarch, and salt; gradually add to chocolate mixture, stirring constantly.
3. Cook and stir over boiling water until thickened. Remove from heat; stir in vanilla extract and butter. Pour into serving dishes and chill.
4. Serve with **whipped cream** or **whipped dessert topping.**

About 4 servings

Semisweet Chocolate Pudding

1 package (6 ounces) semisweet chocolate pieces
¼ cup water
½ cup firmly packed golden brown sugar
4 egg yolks
1 teaspoon vanilla extract
4 egg whites
1 cup chilled whipping cream
2 tablespoons golden brown sugar
Sliced almonds

1. Combine chocolate pieces, water, and ½ cup brown sugar in the top of a double boiler. Heat over simmering water until chocolate is melted. Beat until smooth. Cool.
2. Beat egg yolks with vanilla extract. Stir into chocolate mixture. Beat egg whites until stiff. Fold chocolate mixture into egg whites. Spoon into individual serving dishes. Chill 3 hours.
3. Combine whipping cream and 2 tablespoons brown sugar. Whip until stiff. Top pudding with the whipped cream and sprinkle with almonds.

6 servings

Crunchy Caramel Pudding Parfait

Pudding:
- 1½ cups sugar
- ½ cup boiling water
- 3 tablespoons cornstarch
- 1½ cups milk
- 1 egg, slightly beaten
- 1 teaspoon vanilla extract
- 1 tablespoon butter
- ½ cup chilled whipping cream

Crunch mixture:
- ¼ cup lightly packed brown sugar
- ¼ cup flour
- ¼ cup quick-cooking oats
- ¼ cup finely chopped pecans
- ¼ cup soft butter

1. For pudding, measure 1¼ cups sugar into a heavy saucepan. Heat, stirring constantly, until melted and golden. Remove from heat and add boiling water very carefully while stirring. Return to heat and bring to boiling.

2. Combine cornstarch and milk. Add gradually to caramel syrup, stirring constantly. Bring to boiling over medium heat, stirring occasionally. Cover and cook over low heat 3 to 5 minutes; stir as necessary. Stir a small amount of hot mixture with egg. Blend with mixture in saucepan. Cook 2 minutes, stirring constantly. Mix in vanilla extract and butter. Cover and cool. Chill.

3. Whip cream until soft peaks are formed; beat in remaining ¼ cup sugar. Fold into pudding. Chill.

4. For crunch mixture, combine brown sugar, flour, oats, pecans, and butter; mix until crumbly. Press mixture lightly into an 8-inch square pan.

5. Bake at 350°F 12 to 15 minutes. Crumble into small pieces. Cool.

6. To serve, spoon alternate layers of pudding and crunch mixture into sherbet or parfait glasses.

6 to 8 servings

Danish Raspberry Pudding

- 2 packages (10 ounces each) frozen raspberries
- 3 cups water
- 1 piece (3 inches) stick cinnamon
  Peel of ½ lemon, cut in pieces
- ½ cup sugar
- 6 tablespoons cornstarch
- ½ cup water

1. Combine in a saucepan the raspberries, 3 cups water, cinnamon, and lemon peel. Bring rapidly to boiling; break up block of frozen raspberries with a fork. Boil 5 minutes. Remove from heat. Strain, pressing out liquid. Return liquid to saucepan.

2. Mix sugar with cornstarch. Blend in ½ cup water. Stir into raspberry liquid. Bring to boiling, stirring constantly. Boil 1 minute.

3. Pour mixture into a serving dish. Set aside to cool. Cover; chill thoroughly 3 to 4 hours.

4. Spoon chilled dessert into individual serving dishes and serve with **sugar** and **cream.**

About 10 servings

Meringue-Topped Apricot-Rice Pudding

- 2½ cups milk
- 1 cup white rice, cooked (about 3½ cups)
- 6 tablespoons sugar
- ½ teaspoon salt
- 1 piece (1 inch) vanilla bean
- 1 tablespoon butter
- 3 egg yolks
- 2 tablespoons cream
- 12 to 16 cooked dried apricot halves
- 2 egg whites

1. Scald milk in top of a double boiler over boiling water. Add rice, 6 tablespoons sugar, salt, and vanilla bean piece; mix well. Cover and cook over simmering water 45 minutes. Mix in butter. Blend egg yolks with cream; stir into rice mixture. Set aside to cool.

2. Turn cooled rice pudding into a buttered 9-inch square baking dish. Arrange cooked apricot halves in rows on rice.

3. Beat egg whites until frothy. Add ½ cup sugar gradually, beating until peaks are formed. Using a pastry bag with decorating tube, pipe meringue in swirls over top. Sprinkle with confectioners' sugar.

½ cup sugar
Confectioners' sugar
½ cup red currant jelly
½ cup cooked dried apricot purée

4. Bake at 350°F 15 minutes, or until browned.
5. Melt currant jelly. Decorate between meringue swirls, alternating with currant jelly and apricot purée forced through a pastry bag with tube.

12 to 16 servings

Indian Pudding

3 cups milk
½ cup yellow cornmeal
¼ cup sugar
1 teaspoon salt
1 teaspoon ground cinnamon
½ teaspoon ground ginger
1 egg, well beaten
½ cup molasses
2 tablespoons butter
1 cup cold milk

1. Scald the 3 cups milk in the top of a double boiler. Stirring constantly, slowly blend into milk a mixture of the cornmeal, sugar, salt, cinnamon, and ginger. Stir in a blend of the egg and molasses.
2. Cook and stir over boiling water 10 minutes, or until very thick. Beat in the butter.
3. Turn into a well-buttered 1½-quart casserole. Pour cold milk over top.
4. Bake at 300°F 2 hours, or until browned.

About 6 servings

Quick Indian Pudding

2 eggs, slightly beaten
¼ cup yellow cornmeal
¼ cup sugar
1 teaspoon salt
¾ teaspoon ground cinnamon
¼ teaspoon ground ginger
2 tablespoons cold milk
¼ cup light molasses
2 cups milk, scalded

1. Combine all ingredients except scalded milk in a bowl. Mix well and add the scalded milk gradually, stirring constantly. Turn mixture into a double-boiler top.
2. Cook and stir over direct heat until mixture thickens. Place, covered, over simmering water and cook 15 minutes. Remove cover and cook 15 minutes longer.
3. Serve hot with **ice cream, whipped cream,** or **fruit.**

4 to 6 servings

Rice-Raisin Pudding

5 cups milk
1 cup uncooked white rice
6 tablespoons sugar
1 teaspoon salt
¾ cup golden raisins
Ground cinnamon

1. Heat milk to boiling in a large saucepan. Add rice, sugar, and salt; stir and bring to boiling. Reduce heat and simmer, covered, 45 minutes. Stir in raisins. Continue cooking about 15 minutes, or until rice is entirely soft when a kernel is pressed between fingers, and mixture is very thick and creamy.
2. Remove from heat. Spoon into individual serving dishes and sprinkle lightly with cinnamon. Serve warm.

About 6 servings

Cranberry Pudding with Butter Sauce

1½ cups sifted all-purpose flour
¾ cup sugar
1 tablespoon baking powder
3 tablespoons butter, melted and cooled
1½ cups (about 6 ounces) fresh cranberries, rinsed and coarsely chopped
⅔ cup milk
Butter Sauce

1. Sift the flour, sugar, and baking powder into a bowl. Make a well in center and add the melted butter, cranberries, and milk. Stir just until dry ingredients are moistened.
2. Turn mixture into a greased 1-quart casserole.
3. Bake at 350°F 55 minutes. Serve warm with Butter Sauce.

About 6 servings

Butter Sauce: Melt ½ cup butter in the top of a double boiler. Gradually add 2 cups sugar and ¾ cup half-and-half, stirring frequently, until sugar is completely dissolved, about 15 minutes. Serve with warm pudding.

About 2 cups sauce

Baked Hominy Dessert

1 quart milk
½ cup butter or margarine, cut in pieces
1 cup long-cooking hominy grits
1 teaspoon salt

1. Heat the milk to boiling. Add the butter, then gradually add the hominy grits, stirring constantly. Bring to boiling and boil 3 minutes, or until mixture becomes thick, stirring constantly. Remove from heat.
2. Add the salt; beat at high speed of an electric mixer 5 minutes, or until grits have a creamy appearance.
3. Turn into a buttered 1½-quart casserole.
4. Bake at 350°F 1 hour, or until lightly browned.
5. Serve hot with light brown sugar, cream, and fresh blueberries.

6 to 8 servings

Hawaiian Coconut Pudding (Haupia)

4 cups milk
1½ cups flaked coconut
5 tablespoons cornstarch
6 tablespoons sugar

1. Combine ½ cup of the milk and half the coconut in an electric blender container; blend well. Add an additional 1½ cups milk; blend 5 minutes. Strain out coconut pieces through a double thickness of cheesecloth; reserve coconut. Repeat blending and straining, using remaining coconut and milk.
2. Mix cornstarch with sugar in a saucepan. Gradually add the coconut milk, stirring until smooth. Bring rapidly to boiling and cook 2 to 3 minutes, stirring constantly.
3. Pour into a buttered 8-inch square pan; cool. Refrigerate until firm. Before serving, sprinkle with about ¼ cup of the reserved coconut and cut into squares.

9 servings

Chantilly Raisin-Rice Pudding

⅔ cup seedless raisins
1¼ cups milk
1¼ cups whipping cream
2 eggs
3 tablespoons sugar
⅛ teaspoon ground nutmeg

1. Combine raisins, milk, and cream in a saucepan; place over low heat.
2. Beat the eggs with the sugar, nutmeg, salt, and vanilla extract until thoroughly blended. Mix with the cooked rice. Stir the hot liquid with raisins into the rice mixture and turn into a 1-quart deep baking dish or casserole.

⅛ teaspoon salt
1 tablespoon vanilla extract
1 cup cooked rice
¼ cup chopped toasted nuts
    (walnuts or pecans)

3. Set in a shallow pan of hot water in a 350°F oven. Bake 15 minutes, then sprinkle top with nuts and continue baking 15 to 20 minutes, or until custard is barely set in the center of pudding.
4. Remove from oven and set in a pan with cold water to allow pudding to cool quickly and keep custard creamy.
5. Serving pudding warm or cold. Top with **sweetened whipped cream** or **whipped dessert topping**.

8 servings

Torte-Style Cider Pudding

7 egg yolks
1½ cups sugar
2 teaspoons grated lemon peel
4 cups toasted coarse bread crumbs
1 teaspoon ground cinnamon
1 cup chopped toasted almonds
7 egg whites
1½ cups sweet apple cider

1. Beat the egg yolks, sugar, and lemon peel together until very thick.
2. Combine the bread crumbs, cinnamon, and almonds; fold into the egg-yolk mixture.
3. Beat egg whites until stiff, not dry, peaks are formed. Gently fold into bread-crumb mixture. Turn into a well-greased 9-inch tube pan.
4. Bake at 350°F about 1 hour, or until a cake tester inserted in center comes out clean and top is golden brown.
5. Loosen from sides of pan and then unmold immediately onto a warm serving plate.
6. Heat the cider and pour slowly over the pudding, using just enough to saturate it thoroughly. Serve immediately with **whipped cream**.

12 to 16 servings

Orange Marmalade Pudding

1 cup butter or margarine
1 cup sugar
4 eggs, well beaten
1 cup orange marmalade
1 cup sifted all-purpose flour
1 teaspoon baking soda
    Vanilla Sauce (page 89)

1. Cream butter until softened. Add sugar gradually, beating until thoroughly blended. Add eggs in thirds, beating thoroughly after each addition, until mixture is light and fluffy. Beat in marmalade.
2. Mix flour and baking soda thoroughly and add to butter mixture in fourths, beating only until blended after each addition.
3. Turn into a greased 2-quart mold or 2-pound coffee can. Cover tightly with greased cover, or tie on greased aluminum foil, parchment paper, or double thickness of waxed paper.
4. Place mold on trivet or rack in a large kettle or steamer. Steam 2 hours, following instructions given in step 5 of Molasses Steamed Pudding (page 18).
5. Remove from steamer and unmold onto warm serving dish. Serve with Vanilla Sauce.

About 8 servings

Bread Pudding Puff

2 cups diced firm white bread
  (slightly dry)
1 cup golden raisins
4 eggs
3 cups milk
⅓ cup sugar
1 teaspoon vanilla extract
2 cups sliced peeled peaches

1. Place bread and raisins in a buttered 1½-quart casserole.
2. Combine eggs, milk, sugar, and vanilla extract. Beat until well blended and sugar is dissolved. Pour over bread and raisins.
3. Bake at 350°F 50 to 60 minutes, or until custard is set and top is puffed and browned.
4. Serve warm topped with peaches. If desired, top with whipped cream or vanilla ice cream.

6 to 8 servings

Molasses Steamed Pudding

2 cups sifted all-purpose flour
1 teaspoon baking soda
1 teaspoon salt
1½ teaspoons ground cinnamon
¾ teaspoon ground nutmeg
½ teaspoon ground ginger
¼ teaspoon ground cloves
1 cup buttermilk
¾ cup fine dry bread crumbs
6 ounces suet
½ cup sugar
1 egg, fork beaten
1 cup light molasses
¼ cup water
1 cup chopped nuts
½ cup raisins
Foamy Sauce (page 88)

1. Generously grease a 2-quart mold (or two 1-quart molds). Grease tight-fitting cover. (If cover is not available, aluminum foil, parchment paper, or double thickness of waxed paper cut larger than mold may be substituted. Grease well before tying securely over mold.)
2. Sift the flour, baking soda, salt, and spices together and blend well; set aside.
3. Mix buttermilk and bread crumbs.
4. Pull suet apart, discarding membrane which coats it; put suet through fine blade of food chopper (about 2 cups lightly packed suet). Beat suet until softened in a large mixing bowl; add the sugar and cream thoroughly. Beat in the egg, then the soaked bread crumbs, and a blend of molasses and water. Mix in nuts and raisins, and then the dry ingredients. Turn mixture into mold and cover tightly. Place on a trivet in a steamer or deep kettle with a tight-fitting cover.
5. Pour boiling water into steamer to no more than half the height of the mold. Add more boiling water during steaming, if necessary. Tightly cover steamer. Steam about 3 hours, keeping water boiling gently at all times.
6. Remove pudding from steamer and unmold onto serving plate. Serve with Foamy Sauce.
7. If pudding is to be stored and served later, unmold onto wire rack and cool thoroughly. Wrap in foil or return to the mold and store in a cool place. Before serving, resteam in mold about 3 hours, or until thoroughly heated.

About 12 servings

Lemon Sponge

1 cup sugar
3 tablespoons flour
Few grains salt
2 egg yolks, slightly beaten
2 teaspoons grated lemon peel
2 tablespoons lemon juice
1 tablespoon butter, melted
1 cup milk
2 egg whites

1. Combine sugar, flour, and salt in a bowl; add a mixture of the beaten egg yolks, lemon peel and juice, and melted butter; mix well. Stir in the milk.
2. Beat egg whites until stiff, not dry, peaks are formed. Fold into first mixture. Pour into 6 custard cups.
3. Bake in a pan with hot water in a 350°F oven about 35 minutes, or until golden brown on top. Serve slightly warm.

6 servings

Note: If desired, this sponge may be turned into an unbaked 8-inch pie shell and baked at 350°F 35 to 40 minutes, or until filling is set.

Steamed Pumpkin Pudding

1¼ cups fine dry crumbs
½ cup sifted all-purpose flour
1 cup lightly packed brown sugar
1 teaspoon baking powder
½ teaspoon baking soda
½ teaspoon salt
½ teaspoon ground cinnamon
½ teaspoon ground cloves
2 eggs, fork beaten
1½ cups canned pumpkin
½ cup cooking or salad oil
½ cup undiluted evaporated milk
Lemon Zest Crème

1. Combine bread crumbs, flour, brown sugar, baking powder, baking soda, salt, cinnamon, and cloves in a large bowl. Set aside.
2. Beat eggs and remaining ingredients together. Add to dry ingredients; mix until blended.
3. Turn into a well-greased 1½-quart mold. Cover tightly with a greased cover, or tie greased aluminum foil, parchment paper, or double thickness of waxed paper tightly over mold. Place mold on trivet or rack in a large kettle or steamer.
4. Steam about 3 hours, following instructions given in step 5 of Molasses Steamed Pudding (page 18).
5. Remove pudding from steamer and unmold onto a serving plate. Serve with Lemon Zest Crème.

One 2¼-pound pudding

Lemon Zest Crème: Cream **½ cup butter or margarine** with **½ teaspoon ground ginger** and **¼ teaspoon salt** in a bowl. Add **2 cups confectioners' sugar** gradually, beating constantly. Add **¼ cup lemon juice** gradually, continuing to beat until blended. Mix in **½ cup chopped nuts.**

About 2½ cups crème

Steamed Raisin Pudding

3 cups sifted all-purpose flour
1 teaspoon baking soda
1 teaspoon salt
½ teaspoon ground allspice
½ teaspoon ground cinnamon
½ teaspoon ground nutmeg
¼ teaspoon cloves
4 ounces suet (about 1 cup, chopped)
1 cup molasses
1 cup milk
¼ cup water
1 cup dark seedless raisins
Brown Sugar Pudding Sauce

1. Sift together the flour, baking soda, salt, and spices; set aside.
2. Break apart the suet (discarding membrane which coats it) and finely chop. Combine suet with molasses, milk, and water. Mix in the raisins.
3. Stir in the dry ingredients until well mixed.
4. Turn into a well-greased 2-quart mold. Cover tightly with a greased cover, or tie on greased aluminum foil, parchment paper, or double thickness of waxed paper.
5. Place mold on trivet or rack in a large kettle or steamer. Steam 3 hours, following instructions given in step 5 of Molasses Steamed Pudding (page 18).
6. Remove from steamer and unmold onto a warm serving dish. Serve with Brown Sugar Pudding Sauce.

About 12 servings

Brown Sugar Pudding Sauce: Beat **1 egg, well beaten, 1 cup packed brown sugar,** and **1 teaspoon vanilla extract** until creamy.

About 1 cup sauce

Individual Steamed Chocolate Puddings

1⅓ cups all-purpose flour
1½ teaspoons baking powder
½ teaspoon salt
⅔ cup butter or margarine
2 teaspoons vanilla extract
¾ cup plus 2 tablespoons sugar
2 eggs
3 ounces (3 squares) unsweetened chocolate, melted and cooled
¾ cup milk
1 cup unblanched almonds, toasted and coarsely chopped
Vanilla Hard Sauce (page 88)

1. Combine flour, baking powder, and salt; mix well.
2. Cream butter with vanilla extract until softened; add sugar gradually, beating constantly until blended. Beat in eggs, one at a time, until mixture is fluffy. Blend in the chocolate.
3. Beating just until blended after each addition, alternately add the dry ingredients in fourths and milk in thirds. Stir in almonds.
4. Turn batter into lightly buttered individual molds or small fruit juice concentrate cans, filling each one-half to two-thirds full. Cover molds tightly with aluminum foil and set on rack in steamer. Add boiling water to no more than one half the height of the molds. Cover tightly and steam 30 minutes.
5. Immediately loosen puddings from molds and unmold each onto an individual serving plate. Working quickly, pipe a swirl of Vanilla Hard Sauce on the top of each pudding. Serve immediately before hard sauce melts.

About 8 servings

Chocolate Soufflé

1 tablespoon confectioners' sugar
6 tablespoons butter or margarine
3 ounces (3 squares) unsweetened chocolate
5 tablespoons flour
1½ cups milk
6 egg yolks
⅔ cup sugar
4 teaspoons vanilla extract
6 egg whites

1. Butter bottom of a 1½-quart soufflé dish (straight-sided casserole) and sift the confectioners' sugar over it. Make an aluminum foil collar for soufflé dish (see Note).
2. Melt butter and chocolate together in a heavy saucepan over low heat. Blend in flour. Add milk gradually, blending thoroughly. Stirring constantly, bring to boiling over medium heat. Remove from heat and set aside.
3. Beat egg yolks, sugar, and vanilla extract together until very thick. Add sauce gradually, a spoonful at a time, beating until blended after each addition.
4. Beat egg whites until stiff, not dry, peaks are formed. Spread egg-yolk mixture over egg whites and gently fold together. Turn into soufflé dish. Set in a shallow baking pan with hot water.
5. Bake at 375°F 70 minutes, or until a metal knife inserted halfway between center and edge comes out clean. Lightly sift **confectioners' sugar** over top. Carefully remove collar. Serve immediately.

6 to 8 servings

Note: To make an aluminum foil collar, cut a length of aluminum foil long enough to encircle dish plus 4 or 5 inches. Fold in half lengthwise and wrap around dish so that collar extends at least 2 inches above the rim. Bring the ends together and fold until collar is tight; tie securely with cord.

Double-Boiler Chocolate Soufflé

1 cup milk
2 ounces (2 squares) unsweetened chocolate
3 tablespoons butter or margarine
3 tablespoons flour
½ cup sugar
4 egg yolks
1 teaspoon vanilla extract
4 egg whites
¼ teaspoon cream of tartar

1. Combine milk and chocolate in a saucepan; cook over low heat, stirring occasionally, until chocolate is melted and mixture is blended.
2. Meanwhile, melt butter in a heavy saucepan; stir in the flour and cook until mixture is bubbly. Remove from heat and stir in the milk-chocolate mixture; blend in the sugar. Return to heat and bring the mixture to boiling, stirring constantly.
3. Beat egg yolks until very thick. Adding gradually, beat chocolate mixture into egg yolks until thoroughly blended. Mix in vanilla extract. Cool to lukewarm.
4. Beat egg whites until frothy; add cream of tartar and continue beating until stiff, not dry, peaks are formed. Gently fold in the chocolate mixture until thoroughly blended.
5. Butter inside of top section of a 2-quart metal double boiler; turn mixture into it. Cover and set over boiling water (water should rise to no more than one half of the height of double-boiler top).
6. Keeping water gently boiling, cook 60 to 70 minutes, or until a metal knife inserted halfway between center and edge of soufflé comes out clean.
7. Run a spatula around edge of soufflé and invert onto a serving plate, or spoon into individual serving dishes. Serve immediately; garnish with **sweetened whipped cream.**

About 6 servings

Viennese Chocolate Soufflé

6 egg yolks
¾ cup sugar
10 tablespoons sifted cake flour
2 cups milk
3½ ounces (3½ squares) unsweetened chocolate, grated
1 tablespoon vanilla extract
9 egg whites

1. Beat egg yolks and sugar until very thick in the top of a double boiler. Add the flour gradually, beating until smooth. Gradually add the milk, continuing to beat until blended.
2. Place over rapidly boiling water. Cook and stir 5 minutes, or until thickened. Remove from water; add the chocolate and stir until blended. Mix in vanilla extract. Set on wire rack; allow to stand until mixture cools to lukewarm.
3. Meanwhile, butter a 2-quart soufflé dish (straight-sided casserole). Sprinkle lightly with sugar to coat bottom and sides. Make an aluminum foil collar for soufflé dish (see note following Chocolate Soufflé, page 20).
4. Beat the egg whites until stiff, not dry, peaks are formed and immediately fold with the chocolate mixture. Gently turn into the collared soufflé dish and immediately set in oven on rack (placed so top of product will be about at center of oven).
5. Bake at 375°F 45 to 50 minutes.
6. Remove from oven and carefully remove foil collar. Serve at once with a bowl of Ice-Cream Sauce.

8 to 12 servings

Ice-Cream Sauce: Using equal parts of **vanilla ice cream** and **whipped cream,** fold the cream into softened ice cream just before serving.

Petite Lemon Soufflés

4 egg yolks
¼ cup butter or margarine, softened
¼ cup sugar
Few grains salt
1¼ teaspoons grated lemon peel
¼ cup lemon juice
4 egg whites
¼ cup sugar

1. Put the egg yolks, butter, ¼ cup sugar, salt, and lemon peel and juice into the top of a double boiler; mix well. Cook over simmering water, stirring constantly until thickened (8 to 10 minutes). Remove double-boiler top from water and set aside to cool, stirring occasionally.

2. Beat the egg whites until frothy. Gradually add ¼ cup sugar, beating constantly until stiff peaks are formed. Using a wire whisk, gently blend the egg-yolk mixture into egg whites.

3. Spoon mixture into six 6-ounce heat-resistant glass custard cups. Set in a shallow baking pan, place on oven rack, and pour hot water into pan to a ½-inch depth.

4. Bake at 350°F about 25 minutes, or until tops are lightly browned. Serve immediately.

6 individual soufflés

Soufflé au Grand Marnier et Fruits

½ cup candied fruits
2 tablespoons kirsch
2½ cups milk
1 piece (2 inches) vanilla bean, split
½ cup sugar
⅓ cup flour
⅛ teaspoon salt
4 egg yolks, slightly beaten
¼ cup Grand Marnier
8 egg whites

1. Mix fruits and kirsch; set aside about 2 hours.

2. Scald milk with vanilla bean; cool and strain.

3. Blend sugar, flour, and salt; gradually mix in the scalded milk. Bring to boiling, stirring constantly; cook 3 minutes. Pour slowly into egg yolks, beating constantly until blended; mix in Grand Marnier. Cool to lukewarm.

4. Butter and coat with sugar the bottoms of six 8-ounce baking dishes or individual soufflé dishes.

5. Beat egg whites until stiff, not dry, peaks are formed. Spread egg-yolk mixture over egg whites and carefully fold together.

6. Fill soufflé dishes about one half; distribute fruits over mixture; fill dishes to top with remaining soufflé mixture.

7. With a sharp knife make a small design from center to sides on tops of soufflés. Place in a shallow pan with hot water.

8. Bake at 350°F about 30 minutes, or until tops are lightly browned and a metal knife inserted in soufflés comes out clean.

9. Sprinkle each soufflé with **confectioners' sugar** and, if desired, drizzle with 1 teaspoon Grand Marnier.

6 servings

Chocolate Fondue

4 ounces (4 squares) unsweetened chocolate, cut in pieces
2 cups milk
1¼ cups fine soft bread crumbs
2 tablespoons butter
1 cup sugar
½ teaspoon salt
6 egg yolks, slightly beaten
4 to 6 teaspoons vanilla extract
6 egg whites

1. Heat the chocolate and milk in a large heavy saucepan, stirring until chocolate melts. Remove from heat. Stir in the bread crumbs, butter, sugar, and salt. Blend into the slightly beaten egg yolks in a large bowl. Cool. Stir in vanilla extract.

2. Beat the egg whites until stiff, not dry, peaks are formed. Fold into the cooled chocolate mixture.

3. Turn into a greased (bottom only) 2-quart shallow baking dish. Set in a shallow baking pan with hot water.

4. Bake at 350°F about 40 minutes, or until a knife inserted halfway between center and edge comes out clean.

5. Lightly sift **Dutch process cocoa** over top of fondue and serve warm.

8 servings

Fruit Desserts

Apple Charlotte

6 thin slices white bread
½ cup butter, melted
2 tablespoons butter
6 large apples, cored, pared, and quartered
¼ cup sugar
2 tablespoons lemon juice
1 cup golden raisins
½ cup coarsely chopped pecans

1. Remove crusts from bread slices; cut each into 3 strips. Dip into melted butter; line bottom of a 1½-quart deep glass casserole or ovenproof bowl with strips, then arrange remaining strips upright around sides.
2. Heat 2 tablespoons butter in a skillet; add the apples and cook until apples are tender but not mushy. Sprinkle with sugar and lemon juice. Lightly mix in raisins and pecans. Turn mixture into the bread-lined casserole.
3. Bake at 350°F about 40 minutes, or until bread is golden brown .
4. Cool; unmold and serve with a choice of Apricot Sauce (page 91) or **whipped cream.**

6 to 8 servings

Crustless Apple Pie

⅓ to ½ cup granulated sugar
1 teaspoon cinnamon
1 cup water
6 medium (about 2 pounds) cooking apples, washed, cored, pared, and cut in eighths
1 cup all-purpose flour
1 teaspoon baking powder
Salt (optional)
6 tablespoons shortening
½ cup lightly packed brown sugar

1. Blend granulated sugar and cinnamon in a large, heavy saucepan. Stir in water and apples. Bring to boiling, reduce heat, and cook 10 minutes, stirring occasionally.
2. Meanwhile, blend flour, baking powder, and salt; set aside.
3. Cream shortening with brown sugar until fluffy. Beat in the flour mixture, adding gradually.
4. Turn apples and syrup into a greased 9-inch pie pan. Cover apples completely with the topping.
5. Bake at 350°F about 35 minutes, until apples are tender and topping is browned. Cool on rack.
6. Serve hot or cold with **whipped cream.**

One 9-inch pie

Apple Brown Betty

4 cups diced apples
½ cup firmly packed brown sugar
4 cups cubed coffee cake (slightly dry)
1 cup granulated sugar
½ teaspoon cinnamon
Grated peel and juice of 1 lemon
½ cup water
½ cup coarse bread crumbs
¼ cup butter, melted

1. Generously butter a 1½-quart deep round baking dish. Cover bottom with a layer of apples and sprinkle with about a third of brown sugar. Cover with half of the cubed coffee cake.
2. Combine granulated sugar, cinnamon, and lemon peel; sprinkle half of mixture over coffee cake layer.
3. Cover with a second layer of apples; sprinkle with half of remaining brown sugar; cover with remaining cubed cake, sugar-cinnamon mixture, and sprinkle with a blend of lemon juice and water.
4. Cover with remaining apples, brown sugar, and bread crumbs tossed with melted butter.
5. Cover and bake at 350°F 30 to 40 minutes. Uncover and bake 10 minutes longer, or until golden brown on top.
6. Serve with your favorite lemon sauce.

6 to 8 servings

Danish Apple Cake

2 to 3 pounds apples, cored, pared, and sliced
¼ cup water
½ cup sugar
⅓ cup butter
2½ cups coarse dry bread crumbs
1 cup chilled whipping cream, whipped

1. Cook apples in a covered heavy saucepan with the water and half of the sugar until soft (about 20 minutes).
2. Heat the butter in a heavy skillet. Add the remaining sugar and bread crumbs. Stir over low heat about 5 minutes, or until crumbs are golden brown and crisp.
3. Turn one third of the crumbs into a 1½-quart glass serving dish. Cover with about half the applesauce; continue layering, ending with crumbs.
4. Spoon the whipped cream onto the cake to form a border and decorate with spoonfuls of **jelly** or **jam.** Serve while still warm.

About 8 servings

Apricot Crisp

3 cans (17 ounces each) apricot halves, drained
¼ cup sugar
2 tablespoons flour
½ teaspoon ground cinnamon
¼ teaspoon ground mace
½ cup quick-cooking oats
½ cup all-purpose flour
½ cup firmly packed brown sugar
½ cup butter or margarine

1. Cut apricot halves in quarters and put into a 1½-quart baking dish. Combine sugar, 2 tablespoons flour, cinnamon, and mace. Sprinkle over apricots and mix lightly. Set aside.
2. Combine oats, ½ cup flour, and brown sugar. Using a pastry blender or two knives, cut in the butter until mixture is crumbly. Spoon mixture evenly over apricots.
3. Bake at 350°F 45 minutes, or until mixture is bubbly and top is lightly browned.
4. Serve warm with **cream** or **whipped cream.**

About 8 servings

Maple-Walnut Apple Cream

4 cups chopped Red or Golden
    Delicious apples
2 tablespoons lemon juice
1 cup chilled whipping cream
3 tablespoons maple syrup
½ cup chopped walnuts

1. Toss apples with lemon juice in medium mixing bowl.
2. Beat whipping cream in a small chilled bowl until thickened. Add maple syrup and continue beating until stiff peaks are formed.
3. Mix walnuts with apples and fold into whipped cream. Chill until ready to serve.

6 to 8 servings

Crumb-Coated Bananas with Caramel Topping

6 to 8 medium bananas, peeled and
    cut crosswise into halves
    Frozen orange juice concentrate,
    thawed
¾ cup packaged corn flake crumbs
2 tablespoons butter or margarine
1 egg, slightly beaten
1 jar (11 ounces) caramel topping
2 tablespoons butter or margarine

1. Coat bananas with orange juice concentrate. Combine corn flake crumbs with 2 tablespoons butter. Dip bananas in crumbs, then in slightly beaten egg, and again in crumbs. Place in a shallow baking dish.
2. Bake at 350°F about 10 minutes, or until bananas are tender.
3. While bananas are baking, thoroughly heat the caramel topping with 2 tablespoons butter in a saucepan. Stir to blend and serve sauce over bananas.

6 to 8 servings

Cinnamon-Banana Roll-Ups

2 tablespoons butter or margarine,
    melted
1 teaspoon grated lemon peel
1 teaspoon sugar
8 wedge-shaped pieces of dough
    prepared from crescent-style
    refrigerated rolls or pastry dough
    Finely chopped blanched almonds
    (optional)
8 firm small to medium bananas,
    peeled
    Butter-Cinnamon Mixture I or II
    Flaked coconut (optional)
    Puréed fruit or hot caramel sauce
    (optional)

1. Combine butter with lemon peel and sugar. Brush lightly over the wedges of dough. If desired, press some chopped almonds into the dough.
2. Roll bananas in one of the butter-cinnamon mixtures. Then, if desired, roll the bananas in coconut or chopped almonds.
3. Place each banana on the long point of the wedge of dough. Roll up and place in an ungreased shallow baking pan.
4. Bake at 375°F about 13 minutes, or until rolls are delicately browned.* Serve immediately. If desired, accompany with sauce.

8 banana roll-ups

*For roll-ups using pastry dough, bake at 450°F until pastry is lightly browned.

Butter-Cinnamon Mixture I: Melt ½ **cup butter or margarine** in a saucepan. Stir in **1 tablespoon lemon juice**, ¾ **cup sugar,** and 1½ **teaspoons cinnamon.** Pour mixture into a shallow dish.

Butter-Cinnamon Mixture II: Melt ½ **cup butter or margarine** in a saucepan. Stir in **3 tablespoons brown sugar** and **4 teaspoons cinnamon.** Pour into a shallow dish.

Blueberry Dessert Pizza

1 **package active dry yeast**
¼ **cup warm water**
½ **cup scalded milk**
¼ **cup sugar**
1 **teaspoon salt**
2 **tablespoons soft butter or margarine**
2 **eggs**
1 **teaspoon vanilla extract**
3 **to 3¼ cups all-purpose flour**
 Cream Cheese Filling
 Blueberry Topping

1. Soften yeast in warm water; set aside.
2. Combine scalded milk, sugar, salt, and butter in a large bowl; cool to lukewarm.
3. Stir eggs, vanilla extract, and softened yeast into lukewarm milk mixture. Beat in enough flour to form a dough, beating well after each addition. Cover. Let rise in a warm place until doubled (about 1 hour).
4. Divide dough in half. Roll out each half on a lightly floured surface to form a round 1 inch larger than an inverted 13-inch pizza pan. Place each in a well-greased pizza pan. Fold edges under to form a standing rim; flute.
5. Spread half of filling over each pie. Drop topping onto cheese mixture by the teaspoonful. Let pizzas rise again, uncovered, until doubled (30 to 40 minutes).
6. Bake at 375°F 15 to 20 minutes, or until crust is brown. Sprinkle with confectioners' sugar, if desired.

Two 13-inch dessert pizzas

Cream Cheese Filling: Beat **8 ounces cream cheese** until fluffy. Blend in ⅓ **cup sugar, 1 tablespoon flour, 1 or 2 eggs,** and **1 teaspoon vanilla extract.**

Blueberry Topping: Combine ½ **cup sugar** and **3 tablespoons cornstarch** in a heavy saucepan. Add **1 package (12 ounces) frozen blueberries.** Cook and stir until thick. Stir in **1 tablespoon lemon juice** and **1 tablespoon butter.** Set aside to cool.

Fresh Blueberry "Cobbler"

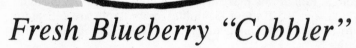

¾ **cup firmly packed light brown sugar**
3 **tablespoons quick-cooking tapioca**
¼ **teaspoon salt**
¼ **teaspoon cinnamon**
 Few grains ground cloves
2 **pints fresh blueberries, rinsed and drained**
1 **tablespoon lemon juice**
2 **tablespoons butter or margarine**
 Pastry for 2-crust pie

1. Combine brown sugar, tapioca, salt, cinnamon, and cloves; mix well. Toss with blueberries until thoroughly mixed. Drizzle lemon juice over berries. Turn into a 10-inch pie plate. Dot with butter; set aside.
2. Prepare pastry. Shape into a ball and flatten on a lightly floured surface. Roll into a rectangle about ⅛ inch thick. Cut pastry diagonally into strips with a pastry wheel or knife, cutting one long strip 2 inches wide to use around edge of pie plate; cut remaining strips ½ inch wide.
3. Form a lattice design over berries. Arrange wider strip around edge so that it extends about ½ inch beyond rim of pie plate. Fold edge of wide strip under strips of pastry and flute edge.
4. Bake at 425°F about 30 minutes, or until golden brown.
5. Serve warm or cool. If desired, garnish cobbler with additional fresh berries placed between lattice strips.

6 to 8 servings

Lemon Crunch Dessert

Lemon mixture:
- ¾ cup sugar
- 2 tablespoons flour
- ⅛ teaspoon salt
- 1 cup water
- 2 eggs, well beaten
- 1 teaspoon grated lemon peel
- ⅓ cup lemon juice

Crunch mixture:
- ½ cup butter or margarine
- 1 cup firmly packed brown sugar
- 1 cup all-purpose flour
- ½ teaspoon salt
- 1 cup whole wheat flakes, crushed
- ½ cup finely chopped walnuts
- ½ cup shredded coconut, finely chopped

1. For lemon mixture, mix sugar, flour, and salt in a heavy saucepan; add water gradually, stirring until smooth. Bring mixture to boiling and cook 2 minutes.
2. Stir about 3 tablespoons of hot mixture vigorously into beaten eggs. Immediately blend into mixture in saucepan. Cook and stir about 3 minutes.
3. Remove from heat and stir in lemon peel and juice. Set aside to cool.
4. For crunch mixture, beat butter until softened; add brown sugar gradually, beating until fluffy. Add flour and salt; mix well. Add wheat flakes, walnuts, and coconut; mix thoroughly.
5. Line bottom of an 8-inch square baking pan with a third of the crunch mixture. Cover with the lemon mixture, spreading to form an even layer. Top with remaining crunch mixture.
6. Bake at 350°F 40 minutes, or until lightly browned. Serve warm or cold.

About 8 servings

Old-fashioned Peach Cobbler

- 1 cup lightly packed brown sugar
- 4 teaspoons cornstarch
- 6 cups sliced fresh peaches
- 3 whole cloves
- 1 piece (3 inches) stick cinnamon
- 1½ cups all-purpose flour
- 3 tablespoons granulated sugar
- 2½ teaspoons baking powder
- ½ teaspoon salt
- ⅓ cup chilled butter
- 1 teaspoon grated lemon peel
- ¾ cup milk
- 1¼ cups half-and-half
- 2 tablespoons brandy (optional)

1. Combine brown sugar and cornstarch in a saucepan. Stir in peaches, cloves, and cinnamon. Cook over medium heat, stirring constantly, until mixture is clear and comes to boiling. Cover and continue to cook over low heat 5 minutes, stirring occasionally. Remove spices. Cover and keep warm.
2. Blend flour, granulated sugar, baking powder, and salt in a bowl. Cut in butter until particles are fine. Add lemon peel and milk; mix lightly with a fork until just combined. Bring fruit mixture to boiling and pour into a 2-quart shallow baking dish. Drop tablespoons of batter onto fruit mixture, spacing evenly.
3. Bake at 400°F about 30 minutes. To serve, pour half-and-half (mixed with brandy, if desired) over individual servings of warm cobbler.

6 to 8 servings

Peaches with Lime Cream

- 1 can (29 ounces) peach halves, drained (reserve ½ cup syrup)
- ⅓ cup firmly packed brown sugar
- Few grains salt
- ⅓ cup orange juice
- 2 tablespoons lime juice
- 2 tablespoons confectioners' sugar
- Few drops vanilla extract
- 1 tablespoon lime juice
- ½ cup chilled whipping cream, whipped
- 1 teaspoon grated lime peel

1. Combine reserved peach syrup, brown sugar, salt, orange juice, and 2 tablespoons lime juice in a heavy skillet. Stirring constantly, cook over low heat until sugar is dissolved.
2. Add peach halves and simmer 15 minutes, turning peaches several times.
3. Blend confectioners' sugar, vanilla extract, and 1 tablespoon lime juice into whipped cream.
4. Spoon warm peaches and syrup into individual serving dishes. Top with whipped cream and sprinkle with lime peel.

About 6 servings

Peaches à l'Orange

¼ cup firmly packed brown sugar
1½ teaspoons cornstarch
1 tablespoon grated orange peel
Few grains salt
1 can (29 ounces) peach halves, drained (reserve ½ cup syrup)
½ cup orange juice
8 whole cloves
6 whole allspice

1. Combine sugar, cornstarch, orange peel, and salt in a saucepan. Add the reserved peach syrup and orange juice gradually, stirring constantly; mix in the cloves and allspice.
2. Bring to boiling, stirring constantly. Add the peach halves and simmer 5 minutes; turning peaches several times.
3. Serve warm or chilled.

About 6 servings

Sherried Peaches

2 cans (16 ounces each) cling peach halves
¼ cup butter or margarine
1 teaspoon lemon juice
¾ cup firmly packed brown sugar
¼ cup sherry
Whipped cream
Nutmeg

1. Drain the peaches, reserving ⅓ cup syrup. Melt the butter in a large saucepan. Stir in the peach syrup, lemon juice, and brown sugar. Bring to boiling.
2. Add peaches and simmer 10 minutes, basting often. Stir in sherry and simmer 5 more minutes.
3. Serve peaches warm, topped with whipped cream and a dash of nutmeg.

6 servings

Orange Baked Pears

1 tablespoon butter or margarine, melted
⅓ cup orange zwieback crumbs (about 4 slices)
3 tablespoons light brown sugar
½ teaspoon grated orange peel
Few grains mace
Few grains salt
1 can (29 ounces) pear halves, drained (reserve syrup)
Plantation Orange Sauce

1. Combine melted butter, zwieback crumbs, brown sugar, orange peel, mace, and salt; mix well.
2. Arrange pears, cut side up, in a shallow baking dish; fill hollows of pears with crumb mixture.
3. Pour ½ cup of the reserved pear syrup around pears; cover with aluminum foil.
4. Bake at 350°F 15 minutes; uncover and bake 15 minutes longer, or until crumbs are browned.
5. Serve warm with Plantation Orange Sauce.

About 8 servings

Plantation Orange Sauce: Blend **3 ounces softened cream cheese** with **2 tablespoons cream** in a bowl. Beat in **¾ teaspoon grated orange peel**, **1 tablespoon orange juice**, and **4 teaspoons confectioners' sugar** until thoroughly blended. Chill 30 minutes.

About ½ cup sauce

Pears Flambée

½ cup dried apricots
2½ cups water
1 cup sugar
1 teaspoon vanilla extract
6 firm ripe pears

1. Put apricots and ½ cup water into a saucepan and set over low heat; cover, and cook slowly about 25 minutes, or until tender. Purée through a sieve and set aside.
2. Combine remaining water with sugar in a large saucepan. Bring to boiling and boil about 5 minutes, stirring until sugar is dissolved. Remove from heat and stir in vanilla extract.
3. Rinse, halve, and carefully remove the core from the pears. Poach them in the syrup over medium heat, simmering about 5 minutes, or until just tender. Carefully remove from syrup. Allowing 2 halves per serving, spoon into individual dishes.
4. Blend the apricot purée into the syrup. Simmer, stirring until sauce is desired thickness. Spoon apricot sauce over pears.
5. Heat ¼ **to ½ cup brandy.** Ignite and pour while flaming over the pears.

6 servings

Pear-Bacon Crisp

6 cups sliced firm ripe pears
2 tablespoons lemon juice
½ cup flaked coconut
½ cup all-purpose flour
¼ cup sugar
¼ cup packed brown sugar
¼ teaspoon salt
1 teaspoon cinnamon
½ teaspoon ground nutmeg
6 slices bacon, diced and fried until crisp (reserve 2 tablespoons drippings)
2 tablespoons butter or margarine, softened
Flaked coconut

1. Sprinkle pears with lemon juice. Toss with coconut. Put half of the pears into a greased 2-quart casserole.
2. Mix flour, sugars, salt, cinnamon, and nutmeg. Blend in reserved drippings and butter. Stir in bacon. Sprinkle half the mixture over pears, add remaining pears, and sprinkle with flour mixture.
3. Bake at 350°F 50 minutes, or until tender.
4. Garnish each serving with coconut.

8 servings

Peaches 'n' Cream Kuchen

2 cups all-purpose flour
2 tablespoons sugar
½ teaspoon salt
¼ teaspoon baking powder
½ cup butter or margarine
9 fresh peach halves, peeled
¾ cup sugar
1 teaspoon cinnamon
2 egg yolks, slightly beaten
1 cup dairy sour cream

1. Combine the flour, 2 tablespoons sugar, salt, and baking powder in a bowl; mix well. Using a pastry blender or two knives, cut in butter until mixture resembles cornmeal.
2. Turn mixture into an 8×8×2-inch baking pan. Pat mixture evenly over bottom and halfway up sides of the pan.
3. Place peach halves, cut side up, in pan. Sprinkle a mixture of the ¾ cup sugar and cinnamon over the peaches.
4. Bake at 400°F 15 minutes. Combine the egg yolks and sour cream; mix thoroughly. Pour over peaches and bake 25 minutes longer.

6 servings

Purple Plum Crunch

5 cups pitted, quartered fresh purple plums
¼ cup packed brown sugar
3 tablespoons flour
½ teaspoon cinnamon
1 cup sifted all-purpose flour
1 cup sugar
1 teaspoon baking powder
¼ teaspoon salt
¼ teaspoon ground mace
1 egg, well beaten
½ cup butter, melted and cooled
1 cup whipping cream
1 teaspoon mace or ½ teaspoon cinnamon

1. Put plums into an ungreased 2-quart shallow baking dish. Sprinkle with a mixture of brown sugar, 3 tablespoons flour, and cinnamon; mix gently with a fork.
2. To prepare topping, sift together 1 cup flour, sugar, baking powder, salt, and mace. Add to the beaten egg and stir with a fork until mixture is crumbly; sprinkle evenly over plums in baking dish. Pour the melted butter evenly over top.
3. Bake at 375°F 40 to 45 minutes, or until topping is lightly browned.
4. Beat whipping cream until stiff, beating in mace with last few strokes. Serve Purple Plum Crunch warm topped with the whipped cream.

6 to 8 servings

Nutty Prune Squares

Filling:
2 pounds dried prunes, rinsed
Juice and grated peel of ½ lemon
1 cup strawberry or raspberry jam

Dough:
3 cups all-purpose flour
1 cup sugar
1 teaspoon baking powder
¼ teaspoon salt
1 cup unsalted butter
1 egg
3 egg yolks
Juice and grated peel of ½ lemon
1 cup finely chopped walnuts

1. To make filling, cook prunes until soft in water in a covered saucepan. Cool prunes, remove and discard pits, cut into halves, and force through a food mill. Mix in lemon juice, peel, and jam.
2. To make dough, mix flour, sugar, baking powder, and salt in a bowl. Cut in butter with pastry blender or two knives until particles are the size of small peas. Add egg, egg yolks, and lemon juice and peel. Mix with a fork until a dough is formed.
3. Divide dough so one portion is enough to cover just the bottom of a 13×9-inch pan. Press dough into pan. On a lightly floured surface, use hands to roll remaining dough into pencil-thin strips.
4. Spoon filling into pan over dough. Sprinkle with walnuts. Make a crisscross effect with dough strips on top of filling.
5. Bake at 350°F until golden brown. Cool. Cut into squares.

12 servings

Berries and Cream

1 quart fresh, ripe strawberries, raspberries, or blueberries
1 cup chilled whipping cream
3 tablespoons confectioners' sugar
1 teaspoon vanilla extract

1. Rinse and hull strawberries; dry thoroughly. Cover and chill.
2. Whip cream, using a chilled bowl and chilled beaters, until it forms soft peaks. Add sugar and vanilla extract and beat to form stiff peaks.
3. Spoon whipped cream into parfait glasses and layer with strawberries, ending with a strawberry on top.

6 servings

Prune Shortbread Dessert

Crust:
- ¾ cup all-purpose flour
- ⅓ cup firmly packed brown sugar
- ⅓ cup butter or margarine

Top layer:
- 2 eggs
- 1 cup firmly packed brown sugar
- 1 teaspoon vanilla extract
- ¼ cup all-purpose flour
- 1 teaspoon baking powder
- ½ teaspoon salt
- ¼ teaspoon ginger
- 1 cup pitted prunes, snipped into small pieces
- ½ cup chopped walnuts
- ½ cup flaked coconut

1. To make crust, combine flour and brown sugar. Cut in butter with a pastry blender or two knives until particles are fine. Press mixture firmly into an even layer in a lightly greased 8-inch square baking pan.
2. Bake at 350°F 10 to 12 minutes, or until edges are lightly browned. Set aside.
3. To make top layer, beat eggs with brown sugar and vanilla extract until light. Sift flour with baking powder, salt, and ginger; blend into egg mixture.
4. Fold in prunes, walnuts, and coconut. Pour over crust, spreading evenly.
5. Bake at 350°F 25 to 35 minutes. Cut into squares when cool. Serve topped with **whipped cream** or **vanilla ice cream**.

9 servings

Baked Rhubarb with Pastry Topping

- 1½ pounds tender pink rhubarb, cut in 1-inch pieces (about 6 cups)
- 1¼ to 1½ cups sugar
- ¾ teaspoon cinnamon
- 1½ teaspoons grated lemon peel
- 1 tablespoon lemon juice
- Pastry for 1-Crust Pie (page 62)
- 2 tablespoons sugar
- ½ teaspoon ground cinnamon

1. Toss rhubarb with 1¼ to 1½ cups sugar, cinnamon, and lemon peel in a 1½-quart shallow baking dish. Drizzle with lemon juice.
2. Prepare pastry and roll out 1 inch larger than overall size of baking dish. Cut slits near center to allow steam to escape.
3. Moisten rim of dish with cold water. Carefully place pastry over rhubarb and trim edge, allowing ½ inch to hang over sides. Fold edge under and press gently to seal. Flute edge. Sprinkle entire surface with a mixture of remaining sugar and cinnamon.
4. Bake at 450°F 10 minutes; turn oven control to 325°F and bake 15 minutes.
5. Serve warm with **whipped dessert topping**.

6 to 8 servings

Springtime Rhubarb Ambrosia: Follow step 1 of recipe for Baked Rhubarb with Pastry Topping; omit pastry and remaining sugar and cinnamon. Cover and cook in a 350°F oven 20 to 25 minutes, or until tender.

Strawberries Romanoff

- 1½ pints ripe strawberries
- 2 to 3 tablespoons granulated sugar
- 2 tablespoons curaçao
- 1 large orange, grated peel and juice
- Sweetened Whipped Cream (page 93)

1. Rinse and hull the strawberries; dry thoroughly. Combine granulated sugar, curaçao, orange juice, and orange peel. Pour over strawberries, mixing gently. Chill several hours.
2. Place chilled strawberries and juice in individual serving dishes. Top generously with the whipped cream.

4 servings

Note: If desired, arrange marinated strawberries over vanilla ice cream in individual serving dishes. Garnish with whipped cream.

Fruit Combo

1 can (16 ounces) fruit cocktail
1 can (8¼ ounces) crushed pineapple
1 can (11 ounces) mandarin oranges
1 package (3¾ ounces) instant vanilla
    pudding and pie filling
2 cups miniature marshmallows
½ cup whipped dessert topping

1. Combine fruits and their juices in a bowl. Stir in pudding and pie filling until well mixed. Fold in marshmallows and whipped topping.
2. Refrigerate 2 to 3 hours or longer. Spoon into sherbet glasses and serve.

8 servings

Cherries Jubilee

1 can (17 ounces) dark sweet
    cherries
1 quart vanilla ice cream
⅓ cup brandy

1. Drain cherries thoroughly, reserving syrup. Pour syrup in chafing dish and bring to boiling over direct heat. Boil about 10 minutes, or until syrup is slightly thickened.
2. Stir in the drained cherries, and place chafing dish over simmering water or low heat until cherries are thoroughly heated. Gently move cherries in pan occasionally and baste with syrup.
3. When ready to serve, heat brandy in a small saucepan. While brandy is heating, spoon ice cream into chilled individual serving dishes.
4. Ignite warm brandy with a match and pour over the cherries. Immediately spoon flaming cherries over the ice cream and serve while flaming.

6 to 8 servings

Rum-Raisin-Apple Flambée

3 large tart apples, pared, cored, and
    thinly sliced
2 tablespoons lemon juice
¼ cup butter
¼ cup firmly packed brown sugar
¼ teaspoon cinnamon
¼ teaspoon nutmeg
¼ cup golden raisins
¼ cup rum
    Vanilla ice cream

1. Sprinkle apple slices with lemon juice to prevent browning.
2. Melt butter in a chafing dish over low direct heat. Stir in brown sugar and spices. Add apples and raisins to pan.
3. Cook mixture 8 to 10 minutes, or until the apples are glazed and tender, but not mushy. Place chafing dish over simmering water or low heat.
4. Heat rum in a small pan, ignite, and pour over apples. Ladle liquid over fruit until flames die. Serve warm over vanilla ice cream.

4 servings

Fresh Fruit with Lemon Sauce

⅓ cup sugar
1 tablespoon cornstarch
⅛ teaspoon salt
1 cup water
½ teaspoon grated lemon peel
2 tablespoons lemon juice
1 teaspoon vanilla extract
½ cup diced fresh, drained canned,
    or thawed frozen, peaches
½ cup fresh or thawed frozen
    blueberries
½ cup seeded red grapes, halved, or
    seedless green grapes

1. Combine sugar, cornstarch, and salt in a saucepan. Blend in water; cook and stir until mixture comes to boiling and is thickened. Remove from heat. Blend in lemon peel and juice and vanilla extract; cool.
2. Mix in fruit, chill, and serve plain or as a topping for cake or pudding.

4 to 6 servings

Pear-Cheese Holiday Mold, 37
Cranberry Jelly Candy, 84
Pastel Candied Fruit Peel, 8

Refrigerator Desserts

Fiesta Melon Mold

5 teaspoons unflavored gelatin
1 cup orange juice
½ cup water
½ cup sugar
¼ cup lime juice
1¾ cups watermelon juice (press pulp against sides of a fine sieve to extract juice)
¼ teaspoon salt
¾ to 1 cup cantaloupe balls
¾ to 1 cup honeydew melon balls
Frosted Grapes

1. Soften gelatin in the orange juice; set aside.
2. Combine water and sugar in a small saucepan. Bring rapidly to boiling, stirring until sugar is dissolved. Boil 3 minutes. Remove from heat; add softened gelatin and stir until gelatin is dissolved. Blend in the remaining fruit juices and salt.
3. Chill until mixture is slightly thickened, stirring occasionally.
4. Stir in the melon balls. Turn mixture into a 1½-quart mold. Chill until firm.
5. To serve, unmold onto a chilled plate and, if desired, accompany with bowls of sweetened whipped cream and chopped salted pecans. Garnish plate with Frosted Grapes.

About 8 servings

Frosted Grapes: Beat **1 egg white** until frothy. Dip small clusters of rinsed, thoroughly drained **grapes** in the beaten egg white. Shake off excess egg white and dip grapes into **granulated sugar.** Set aside to dry. Chill, if desired.

Apricot Snow

½ cup cold water
1 envelope unflavored gelatin
¾ cup sugar
2 cups thick sweetened applesauce
½ cup apricot preserves
2 tablespoons rum
1 teaspoon lemon juice
2 egg whites (unbeaten)

1. Pour cold water into a heavy saucepan. Sprinkle gelatin over it. Stir over low heat until gelatin is dissolved.
2. Remove from heat. Add sugar and stir until dissolved..Mix in applesauce, apricot preserves, rum, and lemon juice.
3. Chill until mixture begins to gel, stirring occasionally. Blend in egg whites. Beat with electric or hand rotary beater until mixture begins to hold its shape. Turn into a 2-quart mold. Chill until firm.
4. Unmold onto a chilled serving plate.

8 servings

Charlotte à l'Orange

11 ladyfingers, split
   Chocolate Glaze
 1 envelope unflavored gelatin
⅔ cup sugar
⅛ teaspoon salt
½ cup water
 1 can (6 ounces) frozen orange juice concentrate, thawed
 1 cup undiluted evaporated milk

1. Line the bottom of a 9-inch pie pan with 5 ladyfingers. Dip remaining ladyfingers into the Chocolate Glaze to coat about one fourth of each. Arrange ladyfingers around edge of pie pan, having chocolate tips uppermost. Drizzle half of remaining glaze over ladyfingers in pan. (Reserve rest of glaze for topping.) Set aside.

2. Combine gelatin, sugar, and salt in a saucepan. Stir in water. Set over low heat, stirring constantly, until gelatin is dissolved.

3. Remove from heat and blend in undiluted orange juice concentrate. Chill until mixture is slightly thickened, stirring occasionally.

4. Pour evaporated milk into a refrigerator tray and place in freezer until ice crystals form around edges. Turn into a chilled bowl and beat until very stiff; fold into gelatin.

5. Turn filling into the pie pan. Drizzle top with remaining Chocolate Glaze. Chill until firm (about 3 hours).

6 to 8 servings

Chocolate Glaze: Partially melt **2 ounces (2 squares) semisweet chocolate** and **2 tablespoons butter** over simmering water, being careful not to overheat. Remove from water and stir until chocolate is completely melted. Cool slightly.

Elegant Chocolate Dessert

 2 ounces (2 squares) unsweetened chocolate
½ cup sugar
¼ cup water
 4 egg yolks, fork beaten
 1 teaspoon vanilla extract
 1 cup unsalted butter
 1 cup confectioners' sugar
 4 egg whites
36 graham crackers

1. Combine chocolate, sugar, and water in the top of a double boiler. Heat and stir over hot water until mixture is slightly thickened and smooth (about 12 minutes).

2. Blend about 3 tablespoons of the mixture into the egg yolks; immediately stir into mixture in double boiler. Cook and stir over boiling water 3 to 5 minutes. Remove from water and blend in vanilla extract. Set aside to cool.

3. When mixture is cooled, cream the butter until softened. Gradually add confectioners' sugar, beating constantly until light and fluffy. Add the chocolate mixture, a small amount at a time, blending well after each addition.

4. Beat egg whites until stiff, not dry, peaks are formed. Fold into chocolate mixture.

5. Use enough graham crackers to cover the bottom of an 8×8×2-inch pan. Spread one third of the chocolate mixture over crackers. Add a second layer of crackers and spread with half of remaining chocolate mixture. Repeat layering and top with graham crackers. Cover and chill about 48 hours.

6. Just before serving, swirl **whipped dessert topping** or **sweetened whipped cream** over top and sprinkle with **shavings of unsweetened chocolate** and **chopped salted pistachio nuts.**

8 or 9 servings

Sunny Citrus Soufflé

2 cups boiling water
2 packages (3 ounces each) lemon-flavored gelatin
1¾ cups lemon-lime carbonated beverage
1 teaspoon grated lemon peel
¼ cup lemon juice
2 cups chilled whipping cream, whipped
Few drops yellow food coloring

1. Tie an aluminum foil collar around top of a 1½-quart soufflé dish (see note following Chocolate Soufflé, page 20). Set aside.
2. Pour boiling water over gelatin in a bowl and stir until dissolved. Add carbonated beverage and lemon peel and juice; blend thoroughly. Chill until mixture is slightly thickened.
3. Beat gelatin until foamy. Fold in whipped cream and food coloring. Spoon mixture into prepared soufflé dish. Chill until firm (about 3 hours).
4. Carefully remove foil collar. Serve chilled with sweetened **fresh strawberries** or Fresh Raspberry Sauce (page 92).

8 servings

Sherry Elegance

3 envelopes unflavored gelatin
1½ cups sugar
3 cups water
1 cup plus 2 tablespoons sherry
¾ cup strained orange juice
⅓ cup strained lemon juice
9 drops red food coloring

1. Combine gelatin and sugar in a large saucepan; mix well. Add water and stir over low heat until gelatin and sugar are dissolved.
2. Remove from heat and blend in remaining ingredients. Pour mixture into a 1½-quart fancy mold or a china serving bowl. Chill until firm.
3. To serve, unmold gelatin onto chilled platter or serve in china bowl without unmolding. Serve with whipped cream or whipped dessert topping, if desired.

6 to 8 servings

Coffee Soufflé Mold

2 envelopes unflavored gelatin
⅔ cup sugar
2¾ cups strong coffee, cooled
1½ cups creamed cottage cheese
1 tablespoon vanilla extract
½ teaspoon salt
2 egg yolks
2 cups chilled whipping cream, whipped
2 egg whites
¼ cup sugar

1. Tie an aluminum foil collar around a 1½-quart soufflé dish (see note following Chocolate Soufflé, page 20). Set aside.
2. Combine the gelatin and ⅔ cup sugar in a saucepan; mix well. Stir in 1 cup of the cooled coffee. Stir over low heat until gelatin and sugar are dissolved. Stir in remaining coffee.
3. Chill until mixture is slightly thickened, stirring occasionally.
4. Meanwhile, force cottage cheese through a food mill or sieve into a bowl. Blend in vanilla extract, salt, and egg yolks.
5. When coffee gelatin is of desired consistency, add gradually to the cottage cheese mixture, beating until well blended. Fold in whipped cream.
6. Beat egg whites until frothy; gradually add ¼ cup sugar, beating constantly until stiff peaks are formed. Spread egg whites over cottage cheese mixture and gently fold together until well blended.
7. Chill until mixture is very thick and piles softly when spooned out.
8. Spoon into soufflé dish and gently level with back of spoon. Garnish top with **grated unsweetened chocolate.** Chill until firm (about 6 hours).
9. When ready to serve, carefully remove foil collar.

8 to 10 servings

Mocha-Caramel Bavarian

1 cup undiluted evaporated milk
1 cup sugar
¾ cup boiling water
1 envelope unflavored gelatin
½ cup cold double-strength coffee
½ teaspoon vanilla extract
⅛ teaspoon salt

1. Pour evaporated milk into a refrigerator tray. Place in freezer until ice crystals form around edges.
2. Melt sugar in a heavy light-colored skillet over low heat, gently moving it with wooden spoon toward center. Heat until golden brown.
3. Remove from heat and, stirring constantly, add the boiling water, a very small amount at a time. Return to low heat and continue stirring until bubbles are the size of dimes.
4. Meanwhile, soften gelatin in cold coffee. Gradually add the cooked syrup to the softened gelatin, stirring constantly; stir until gelatin is dissolved.
5. Stir vanilla extract and salt into the gelatin mixture. Chill until mixture is slightly thickened, stirring occasionally.
6. Turn chilled evaporated milk into a chilled bowl. Beat with an electric mixer on medium speed until stiff peaks are formed.
7. Gently fold into chilled gelatin mixture. Turn into a 1-quart mold. Chill until firm.
8. Unmold onto a chilled serving plate or spoon into chilled sherbet glasses.

6 servings

Vanilla Rice Cream

2 cups boiling water
2 cups milk, scalded
1 tablespoon vanilla extract
½ teaspoon salt
⅔ cup uncooked rice
⅔ cup sugar
1 cup finely chopped toasted filberts
1 envelope unflavored gelatin
½ cup cold water
1 package (3 ounces) whipped topping mix
1 tablespoon vanilla extract
Fresh or frozen strawberries or raspberries

1. Combine boiling water, milk, 1 tablespoon vanilla extract, and salt in a heavy saucepan. Bring to boiling; add the rice gradually, stirring with a fork. Continue to stir 1 minute. Cover and cook over low heat 35 to 45 minutes, stirring occasionally until almost all the liquid is absorbed and rice is tender. Remove from heat and add sugar and filberts. Set aside to cool.
2. Soften gelatin in cold water in a heavy saucepan. Stir over low heat until gelatin is completely dissolved. Chill until mixture is slightly thicker than consistency of thick unbeaten egg white, stirring frequently.
3. Meanwhile, whip topping mix according to package directions. Beat in 1 tablespoon vanilla extract.
4. Stir thickened gelatin into cooled rice-filbert mixture. Blend in the whipped topping.
5. Turn into a 2-quart mold. Refrigerate until firm (at least 3 hours).
6. Unmold onto a chilled serving plate and garnish with strawberries or raspberries.

8 to 10 servings

Lemon Egg Fluff

3 envelopes unflavored gelatin
½ cup sugar
  Few grains salt
1 cup water
10 egg yolks, beaten
1 can (6 ounces) frozen lemonade
    concentrate, thawed
10 egg whites
½ cup sugar
  Cherry-Cinnamon Sauce

1. Thoroughly blend gelatin, sugar, and salt in a heavy saucepan. Mix in water. Stir over low heat until gelatin is dissolved.
2. Gradually add a small amount of hot gelatin mixture to egg yolks, stirring constantly. Blend into mixture in saucepan; cook and stir 2 minutes without boiling.
3. Remove from heat. Stir in lemonade concentrate. Chill until mixture is slightly thickened.
4. Beat egg whites until frothy. Gradually add sugar, continuing to beat until stiff peaks are formed; fold in gelatin mixture. Turn into a 2½-quart tower mold and chill until firm.
5. Unmold onto a chilled serving plate and serve with sauce.

12 servings

Cherry-Cinnamon Sauce: Combine **½ cup sugar** and **2 tablespoons cornstarch** in a saucepan; mix thoroughly. Drain **1 can (about 16 ounces) pitted tart red cherries,** reserving the liquid. Add cherry liquid and **3 tablespoons red cinnamon candies** to sugar mixture. Bring to boiling, stirring constantly; continue cooking until mixture is thickened and clear. Remove from heat. Stir in **1 tablespoon lemon juice** and the cherries. Cool.

About 2¼ cups sauce

Crème Magnifique

1 envelope unflavored gelatin
1 cup sugar
  Few grains salt
2 cups whipping cream
1½ teaspoons vanilla extract
¼ teaspoon almond extract
2 cups dairy sour cream

1. Mix gelatin, sugar, and salt in a heavy saucepan. Stir in whipping cream. Place over low heat and stir until gelatin is completely dissolved. Remove from heat and chill until mixture begins to gel, stirring occasionally.
2. Stir extracts with sour cream; blend with gelatin.
3. Turn into 8 individual molds. Chill until firm.
4. Unmold onto chilled dessert dishes and serve with thawed **frozen raspberries** or **strawberries.**

8 servings

Pear-Cheese Holiday Mold

1 can (29 ounces) pear halves
2 packages (3 ounces each) or 1
    package (6 ounces) lime-flavored
    gelatin
½ teaspoon salt
2 cups boiling water
1 tablespoon lemon juice
1 package (8 ounces) cream cheese,
    softened
⅛ teaspoon ginger
½ cup chopped pecans

1. Drain pears, reserving syrup. Dice pears and set aside. Add enough water to reserved syrup to make 1½ cups liquid.
2. Dissolve gelatin and salt in boiling water. Add pear liquid and lemon juice. Chill half of the gelatin mixture until thickened. Stir in pears and pour into a 6-cup ring mold. Chill until set, but not firm.
3. Chill remaining gelatin until slightly thickened. Combine cream cheese and ginger. Gradually blend in gelatin and beat smooth. Stir in nuts and spoon into mold. Chill until firm (about 4 hours). Unmold onto a serving plate.

12 servings

Creamy Cherry Mold

1 can (29 ounces) pitted dark sweet
    cherries, drained (reserve syrup)
1 package (3 ounces) cherry-flavored
    gelatin
2 cups dairy sour cream

1. Add enough water to reserved cherry syrup to make 2 cups liquid. Heat 1 cup of the liquid to boiling and pour over the gelatin. Stir until dissolved. Stir in remaining liquid. Chill until mixture is slightly thickened, stirring occasionally.
2. Stir in the sour cream. Halve the cherries and stir into gelatin mixture. Turn into a 1½-quart mold and chill until firm.
3. Unmold onto a chilled serving plate.

8 to 10 servings

Cranberry Jeweled Crown

4 cups (1 pound) fresh cranberries,
    rinsed
1 cup cold water
¾ to 1 cup sugar
¾ cup orange juice
1 package (3 ounces) orange-flavored
    gelatin
¼ teaspoon salt
1 cup chilled whipping cream,
    whipped
1 cup chopped walnuts

1. Combine cranberries in a saucepan with the cold water and sugar. Bring to boiling over medium heat and cook until skins of cranberries pop. Force through a sieve or food mill; set aside.
2. Heat orange juice. Combine gelatin and salt in a bowl; add orange juice and stir until gelatin is dissolved.
3. Stir in the sieved cranberries. Cool; chill until mixture is slightly thickened, stirring occasionally.
4. Fold whipped cream and walnuts into gelatin mixture. Turn into a 1½-quart fancy mold. Chill until firm.
5. Unmold onto a chilled serving plate.

6 to 8 servings

Maple Nut Mold

¼ cup cornstarch
¼ cup cold water
2 cups boiling water
1½ cups lightly packed brown sugar
3 egg whites
½ cup chopped walnuts

1. Thoroughly blend cornstarch and water until smooth in a heavy saucepan. Add boiling water gradually, stirring constantly. Mix in the brown sugar. Bring to boiling, continuing to stir. Reduce heat and cook 30 minutes, stirring occasionally.
2. Beat egg whites until stiff, not dry, peaks are formed. Pour hot cornstarch mixture gradually over egg whites, beating constantly until blended. Mix in walnuts.
3. Spoon into individual molds, cover, and chill. Unmold. Serve with **whipped cream.**

6 to 8 servings

Creamy Pineapple Mold

1 envelope unflavored gelatin
1 can (20 ounces) crushed pineapple,
    drained (reserve syrup)
⅓ cup mint-flavored apple jelly
1 cup chilled whipping cream,
    whipped

1. Soften gelatin in ½ cup reserved syrup in a saucepan. Stir over low heat until gelatin is dissolved. Remove from heat; add jelly and stir until melted.
2. Blend in the pineapple with remaining pineapple syrup. Chill until mixture mounds slightly when dropped from a spoon, stirring occasionally.
3. Fold whipped cream into gelatin mixture. Turn into a 5-cup mold. Chill until firm.
4. Unmold on a chilled serving plate and garnish with **fresh mint.**

6 to 8 servings

Pashka

A traditional Russian Easter dessert.

2 packages (8 ounces each) cream
    cheese, softened
1 cup large-curd creamed cottage
    cheese
½ cup butter, softened
½ cup sugar
1 tablespoon finely shredded lemon
    peel
1 tablespoon finely shredded orange
    peel
1 teaspoon vanilla extract
⅓ cup chopped candied red cherries
¼ cup golden raisins
2 tablespoons diced candied
    pineapple
¼ cup chopped toasted almonds
    Candied cherries

1. Combine cheese, butter, sugar, lemon and orange peels, and vanilla extract; beat until smooth. Mix in remaining ingredients.
2. With a moistened piece of cheesecloth, line a thoroughly cleaned flowerpot (5½ inches across top and 5½ inches high) having a drainage hole.
3. Spoon cheese mixture into flowerpot. Place pot on a rack in a shallow pan. Cover and chill, overnight or longer, to allow flavors to blend.
4. Unmold and garnish with whole candied cherries.

10 to 12 servings

Molded Pineapple-Coconut Cream

1 can (8¼ ounces) crushed pineapple,
    drained (reserve syrup)
1 package (3 ounces) lime-flavored
    gelatin
    Few grains salt
2 teaspoons grated lime peel
½ cup lime juice
1 pint vanilla ice cream
¾ cup flaked coconut
    Lime slices, halved

1. Add enough water to reserved pineapple syrup to make 1 cup liquid. Heat to boiling.
2. Mix gelatin and salt in a bowl. Add boiling liquid and stir until completely dissolved. Mix in lime peel and juice. Add ice cream by spoonfuls; blend until smooth. Chill until mixture is slightly thickened, stirring occasionally.
3. Mix in pineapple and coconut. Turn into a 5-cup mold. Cover; chill until firm (about 2 hours).
4. To serve, unmold onto a chilled plate and garnish with half slices of lime.

About 8 servings

Snow Pudding

1 envelope unflavored gelatin
½ cup plus 2 tablespoons sugar
⅛ teaspoon salt
1¼ cups water
¼ cup strained lemon juice
3 egg whites

1. Mix the gelatin, sugar, and salt in a saucepan. Stir in the water. Stir over low heat until gelatin and sugar are dissolved. Remove from heat and stir in the lemon juice.
2. Chill until mixture is slightly thickened, stirring occasionally.
3. When gelatin is of desired consistency, beat egg whites until stiff, not dry, peaks are formed.
4. Beat gelatin mixture until frothy. Fold into the beaten egg whites. Turn into a 1½-quart fancy mold. Chill until firm (about 3 hours).
5. Unmold onto a chilled serving plate and serve with **lingonberry preserves** or Raspberry Sauce (page 92).

About 6 servings

Elegant Strawberry Cream

1½ tablespoons unflavored gelatin
¾ cup sugar
¼ teaspoon salt
1 cup half-and-half
½ cup water
½ teaspoon vanilla extract
1 package (16 ounces) frozen sliced
    strawberries, thawed
1 cup dairy sour cream

1. Mix gelatin, sugar, and salt in a saucepan. Stir in half-and-half and water. Set over low heat and stir until sugar and gelatin are dissolved. Remove from heat and stir in vanilla extract.
2. Cool slightly, then chill until mixture is slightly thickened, stirring occasionally.
3. Beat gelatin with a rotary beater until light and fluffy. Add the strawberries and sour cream and stir lightly until blended. Turn into a 1-quart fancy mold and chill until firm.
4. Unmold dessert onto a chilled serving plate.

About 6 servings

Note: Frozen raspberries may be substituted for strawberries, if desired.

Désir de la Pompadour with English Cream

A recipe from Lasserre Restaurant, Paris, France.

30 ladyfingers
2 egg yolks
2 tablespoons sugar
½ cup butter, softened
4 ounces (4 squares) unsweetened
    chocolate, melted and cooled
½ cup sieved apricot jam
⅓ cup toasted chopped almonds
English Cream

1. Line the bottom of an 8-inch springform pan with 10 ladyfingers. Cut 10 ladyfingers in halves, crosswise, and arrange around side of pan; set aside.
2. Beat the egg yolks and sugar in a bowl until thick. Gradually blend in the butter, beating well. Blend in the melted chocolate.
3. Spread the chocolate mixture over the layer of ladyfingers. Arrange the remaining ladyfingers over the chocolate layer. Spread a thin layer of apricot jam over the top. Sprinkle with almonds. Chill 2 hours.
4. Serve in wedges topped with English Cream.

8 servings

English Cream

1⅓ cups milk
1 piece (2 inches) vanilla bean, split
    lengthwise
3 egg yolks, slightly beaten
6 tablespoons sugar
2 tablespoons kirsch

1. Heat the milk with vanilla bean in a heavy saucepan until scalded. Set aside.
2. Blend the egg yolks and sugar in the top of a double boiler. Remove vanilla bean from milk and gradually add the milk to egg yolk mixture, stirring constantly.
3. Cook and stir over boiling water until mixture coats a metal spoon; do not overcook. Remove from boiling water and cool to lukewarm over cold water. Blend in the kirsch.
4. Refrigerate until ready to serve.

About 1½ cups sauce

Desert Date Roll

3 tablespoons orange juice
¼ teaspoon salt
2 cups graham cracker crumbs
2 cups chopped pitted dates
1¼ cups miniature marshmallows
½ cup chopped walnuts
1 cup chilled whipping cream,
    whipped

1. Mix orange juice and salt with graham cracker crumbs in a large bowl. Stir in dates, marshmallows, and walnuts. Fold in whipped cream; mix well.
2. Turn the mixture onto a large sheet of waxed paper. Shape into a roll about 3 inches in diameter and wrap in waxed paper. Chill overnight.
3. To serve, slice and top with generous dollops of whipped cream.

6 to 8 servings

Apricot Chiffon Dessert

1 can (30 ounces) apricot halves,
    drained (reserve 1¼ cups syrup)
2 tablespoons apricot preserves or
    jam
1 envelope unflavored gelatin
¼ cup sugar
1 tablespoon lemon juice
1 cup chilled whipping cream,
    whipped
¼ teaspoon vanilla extract
¼ teaspoon almond extract
18 vanilla wafers, crushed (⅔ cup)
2 tablespoons butter or margarine,
    melted

1. Force apricots through a sieve or food mill. Stir in apricot preserves or jam; set aside.
2. Mix gelatin and sugar together in a saucepan. Stir in lemon juice and reserved apricot syrup. Stir over low heat until gelatin and sugar are dissolved. Add to the sieved apricots, stirring until thoroughly blended.
3. Chill in refrigerator or over ice and water until mixture is slightly thickened; stir frequently.
4. Blend a mixture of extracts into the whipped cream. Beat the gelatin mixture slightly; fold in whipped cream.
5. Combine crushed vanilla wafers and melted butter; mix thoroughly. Spread about two thirds of the crumbs on the bottom of an 8-inch square pan. Turn the apricot-whipped cream mixture into the pan. Top evenly with remaining crumbs. Chill until firm (about 4 hours).

8 or 9 servings

Strawberry-Cheese Fluff

1 envelope unflavored gelatin
¼ cup sugar
⅛ teaspoon salt
¼ cup cold water
1 package (10 ounces) frozen sliced
    strawberries, thawed and
    drained (reserve syrup)
1 cup dairy sour cream
¾ cup small-curd creamed cottage
    cheese
4 ounces cream cheese, softened

1. Combine gelatin, sugar, and salt in a saucepan. Mix well and stir in the water and ¼ cup of the reserved strawberry syrup. Stir over low heat until gelatin and sugar are dissolved.
2. Combine in a bowl the strawberries, remaining syrup, sour cream, and cheese. Beat until thoroughly blended. Stir in the dissolved gelatin. Pour into a bowl and chill until firm, 8 hours or overnight.
3. To serve, spoon dessert into chilled sherbet glasses. Accompany with a selection of toppings such as **whipped cream, crushed strawberries,** and **flaked coconut.**

About 6 servings

Pineapple Refrigerator Dessert

1 envelope unflavored gelatin
1 can (20 ounces) crushed pineapple, drained (reserve ½ cup syrup)
2 cups chilled whipping cream, whipped
40 graham crackers
¼ cup finely chopped crystallized ginger

1. Soften gelatin in reserved pineapple syrup in a saucepan. Stir over low heat until gelatin is dissolved. Blend into crushed pineapple. Chill until mixture is slightly thickened, stirring occasionally.
2. Fold half of the whipped cream into chilled gelatin mixture until evenly blended.
3. Spread a thin layer of the gelatin mixture on each graham cracker; turn crackers on end and press together to form a loaf.
4. Spread with remaining whipped cream; garnish with ginger. Chill about 3 hours.
5. To serve, cut into diagonal slices.

About 10 servings

Raspberry Fluff

30 marshmallows (about 8 ounces)
⅓ cup orange juice
1 package (10 ounces) frozen raspberries, thawed
1 cup chilled whipping cream, whipped

1. Heat marshmallows and orange juice in the top of a double boiler over boiling water until marshmallows are melted, stirring occasionally. Remove from heat and turn into a bowl; set aside to cool.
2. Stir thawed raspberries with their syrup into cooled marshmallow mixture. Gently fold in whipped cream. Cover and chill 3 to 4 hours.
3. To serve, spoon into parfait glasses.

About 6 servings

Rhubarb Soufflé

1 envelope unflavored gelatin
½ cup sugar
⅛ teaspoon salt
4 egg yolks
½ cup cold water
1½ cups rhubarb purée*
2 tablespoons grenadine
4 egg whites
½ cup sugar
1 cup chilled whipping cream, whipped

1. Tie an aluminum foil collar around a 1-quart soufflé dish (see note following Chocolate Soufflé, page 20). Set aside.
2. Combine gelatin, ½ cup sugar, and salt in the top of a double boiler. Beat egg yolks and water together until thoroughly blended. Stir into gelatin mixture.
3. Set over boiling water and cook about 5 minutes to cook egg yolks and dissolve gelatin, stirring constantly.
4. Remove from heat and stir in the rhubarb purée and grenadine. Cool mixture, then chill until it is slightly thickened, stirring occasionally.
5. Beat egg whites until frothy; add remaining ½ cup sugar, a little at a time, beating constantly until stiff peaks are formed.
6. Fold whipped cream and meringue together. Fold in chilled gelatin mixture until blended. Turn into prepared dish and chill until firm.
7. When ready to serve, carefully remove foil collar.

About 8 servings

*To make rhubarb purée, cook about **3 cups cut-up rhubarb** with about **2 tablespoons water** in a covered heavy saucepan until rhubarb is tender. Force through a sieve or turn into an electric blender container and blend until smooth.

Frozen Desserts

Frozen Chocolate Mousse

⅔ cup sugar
¼ cup water
4 ounces (4 squares) unsweetened chocolate
1½ teaspoons unflavored gelatin
¼ cup cold water
2 cups chilled whipping cream
½ cup confectioners' sugar
1 teaspoon vanilla extract
½ cup chilled whipping cream

1. Put sugar and ¼ cup water into top of a double boiler. Place over direct heat and stir until sugar is dissolved.

2. Set over simmering water and add chocolate. Heat until chocolate is melted. Remove from heat and set aside to cool.

3. Soften gelatin in cold water in a small saucepan. Stir over low heat until gelatin is dissolved.

4. Rinse a fancy 1½-quart mold with cold water and set aside to drain.

5. Beat whipping cream, 1 cup at a time, in a chilled bowl using a chilled rotary beater, until it piles softly. Beat the confectioners' sugar and vanilla extract into the whipped cream until blended.

6. Stir dissolved gelatin into chocolate mixture and gently mix chocolate into whipped cream until thoroughly blended. Spoon into mold, and place in freezer about 3 hours, or until firm.

7. Beat ½ cup whipping cream, using a chilled bowl and chilled beaters, until cream stands in stiff peaks when beater is lifted.

8. Just before ready to serve, remove mousse from freezer. To unmold, loosen top edge of mold with a knife. Wet a clean towel in hot water and wring it almost dry. Place a chilled serving plate on mold and invert. Wrap towel around mold for a few seconds only. Gently remove mold. If mousse does not loosen, repeat.

9. Force whipped cream through a pastry bag and a No. 27 star tube, to decorate center and sides of mousse.

10 to 12 servings

Avocado Ice Cream

3 ripe avocados
½ cup sugar
⅓ cup lime juice
1 quart vanilla ice cream, slightly softened

1. Halve, pit, and peel avocados. Mash avocado in a bowl. Mix in sugar and lime juice.
2. Spoon ice cream onto avocado mixture and beat until smooth. Turn into refrigerator trays and freeze until firm.
3. To serve, spoon into chilled dessert dishes and serve immediately.

About 2½ pints ice cream

Banana-Pecan Ice Cream

3 medium-size firm ripe bananas
1 tablespoon lemon juice
½ cup sugar
¼ teaspoon salt
⅓ cup milk
2 egg yolks
1 teaspoon vanilla extract
2 egg whites
1 cup chilled whipping cream, whipped
½ cup chopped pecans

1. Cut bananas into pieces and put into a blender container with lemon juice, sugar, salt, milk, egg yolks, and vanilla extract; blend until smooth.
2. Beat egg whites until stiff, not dry, peaks are formed. Fold whipped cream into egg whites and blend thoroughly. Stir in the banana mixture.
3. Turn into refrigerator trays; freeze just until mixture begins to thicken (about 1½ hours).
4. Turn into a chilled bowl and beat until creamy and smooth. Stir in the pecans and return to trays. Freeze until firm (about 2 hours).

About 1 quart ice cream

Coconut Ice Cream

½ cup sugar
Few grains salt
1 cup milk, scalded
1 medium-size coconut (about 2½ cups small pieces)
2 cups whipping cream
2 teaspoons vanilla extract
2 tablespoons confectioners' sugar

1. Stir the sugar and salt into the scalded milk until dissolved. Pour into an electric blender container; add a few pieces of the coconut and blend. Continue adding coconut while blending. Finally blend 5 minutes. Mix with 1 cup of the cream and vanilla extract.
2. Pour into refrigerator trays; freeze until mixture is mushy.
3. Whip remaining cup of cream until of medium consistency (piles softly). Beat in confectioners' sugar with final few strokes.
4. Remove the partially frozen mixture from freezer and turn into a chilled bowl. Beat just until smooth. Fold in the whipped cream. Return to trays and freeze until firm.

About 1½ quarts ice cream

Note: Substitute 2 cans (3½ ounces each) flaked coconut for the fresh coconut, if desired. Reduce sugar to 2 tablespoons.

Lemon-Cheese Ice Cream

6 ounces cream cheese
⅔ cup sugar
2 cups cream or half-and-half
2 tablespoons lemon juice
1 teaspoon grated lemon peel
¼ teaspoon vanilla extract

1. Using an electric beater, beat the cream cheese until softened. Gradually add the sugar, beating until fluffy.
2. Add the cream slowly, mixing well. Beat in remaining ingredients until thoroughly mixed. Pour into a refrigerator tray and freeze until mushy.
3. Turn mixture into a chilled bowl and beat with a hand rotary or electric beater until smooth. Return to refrigerator tray and freeze until firm.

About 1 quart ice cream

Haitian Ice Cream

2 cups milk
2 ounces (2 squares) unsweetened chocolate
1 cup sugar
1 tablespoon flour
¼ teaspoon salt
¼ teaspoon ground cloves
3 egg yolks, slightly beaten
2 cups half-and-half
2 teaspoons vanilla extract

1. Combine milk and chocolate in top of a double boiler; heat over boiling water until milk is scalded and chocolate is melted.
2. Combine sugar, flour, salt, and cloves; add gradually to milk mixture, blending well. Cook and stir over direct heat 5 minutes.
3. Remove from heat and vigorously stir about 3 tablespoons of the hot mixture into the egg yolks; immediately stir into hot mixture. Cook over boiling water 10 minutes, stirring constantly, until mixture coats a metal spoon.
4. Remove from heat; cool. Stir in half-and-half and vanilla extract. Pour into refrigerator trays and freeze until mushy.
5. Turn into a chilled bowl and beat with hand rotary or electric beater until smooth and creamy. Return mixture to trays and freeze until firm.

About 1½ quarts ice cream

Coffee Tortoni

2 tablespoons butter or margarine
2 tablespoons sugar
½ cup toasted wheat germ
3 tablespoons finely chopped toasted almonds
1 cup chilled whipping cream
½ cup confectioners' sugar
2 tablespoons instant coffee
2 tablespoons sherry or rum
1 egg white, beaten to soft peaks
4 maraschino cherries, halved

1. Melt butter in a saucepan and stir in sugar. Cook over medium heat until bubbly.
2. Stir in wheat germ and almonds, mixing well. Remove from heat; spread out to cool on waxed paper.
3. Beat whipping cream, confectioners' sugar, and coffee until soft peaks are formed. Fold in ¾ cup of wheat germ mixture, the sherry, and beaten egg white.
4. Spoon into 8 paper baking cups set in muffin-pan wells. Sprinkle remaining ¼ cup wheat germ mixture over all, and top each with a cherry half. Freeze until firm.

8 servings

Mocha-Brazil Nut Ice Cream

1 envelope unflavored gelatin
¾ cup firmly packed light brown sugar
⅛ teaspoon salt
1 tablespoon instant coffee
1¼ cups water
1 ounce (1 square) unsweetened chocolate, cut in small pieces
2 teaspoons vanilla extract
1 can (13 ounces) evaporated milk
1½ cups whipping cream
¾ cup chopped toasted Brazil nuts

1. Mix the gelatin, brown sugar, salt, and instant coffee thoroughly in a saucepan. Stir in water and chocolate. Cook and stir over medium heat until gelatin and sugar are dissolved and chocolate is melted. Remove from heat; set aside to cool.
2. Stir vanilla extract, evaporated milk, and cream into the cooked chocolate mixture. Pour into refrigerator tray. Freeze until mushy.
3. Turn into a chilled bowl and beat with rotary beater until smooth. Return to tray and freeze until partially frozen.
4. Stir in the nuts. Cover top with shaved **unsweetened chocolate** and freeze until firm.

About 1½ quarts ice cream

Creamy Orange Velvet

2 cups sugar
2 cups milk, scalded
2 cups whipping cream
2 tablespoons grated orange peel
¾ cup orange juice
½ cup lemon juice

1. Stir sugar into scalded milk; set aside to cool.
2. Stir cream, orange peel, and orange and lemon juices into milk mixture. Pour into refrigerator trays. Freeze until mushy.
3. Turn mixture into a chilled bowl and beat until smooth, but not melted. Return to trays and freeze until firm.

About 2 quarts ice cream

Pumpkin Ice Cream

1 cup canned pumpkin
⅓ to ½ cup sugar
½ teaspoon ground cinnamon
¼ teaspoon ground ginger
¼ teaspoon ground nutmeg
2 tablespoons orange juice
2 teaspoons vanilla extract
1 cup chilled whipping cream, whipped

Mix pumpkin with sugar, spices, orange juice, and vanilla extract. Fold into whipped cream. Turn into a refrigerator tray; freeze until firm.

About 1½ pints ice cream

Peach Ice Cream Superb

12 medium-size (about 3 pounds) fully ripe peaches, peeled and pitted
2¾ cups sugar
1 tablespoon lemon juice
1½ quarts chilled whipping cream
¼ teaspoon salt
1 teaspoon vanilla extract
1 teaspoon almond extract

1. Wash and scald cover, container, and dasher of a 4-quart ice cream freezer. Chill thoroughly.
2. Force peaches through a sieve or food mill. Stir sugar and lemon juice into peaches and set aside 20 minutes.
3. Combine cream, salt, and extracts; mix with peaches until blended.
4. Fill freezer container two thirds full with ice cream mixture. Cover tightly. Set in freezer tub. (For electric freezer, follow manufacturer's directions.)
5. Fill tub with alternate layers of 8 parts crushed ice and 1 part rock salt. Turn handle slowly 5 minutes. Add crushed ice and rock salt as necessary.

OUR FLAVORS

PEACH VANILLA CHOCOLATE
APRICOT STRAWBERRY • • •

6. Wipe cover free of ice and salt. Remove dasher and pack down ice cream. Cover with moisture-vaporproof material. Replace cover and plug opening for dasher. Repack freezer with alternate layers of ice and salt, using 4 parts ice and 1 part rock salt. Cover with heavy paper or cloth. Let stand 2 to 3 hours to ripen.

About 3 quarts ice cream

Maple Ice Cream Superb: Follow the recipe for Peach Ice Cream Superb. Omit peaches, sugar, lemon juice, and almond extract. Pour 1½ **cups maple syrup** into a medium-size saucepan. Bring rapidly to boiling and boil to reduce to 1¼ cups (about 15 minutes). Remove from heat and cool. Increase vanilla extract to 1 tablespoon and blend with the cream and salt. Add maple syrup gradually, stirring constantly until thoroughly blended.

Chocolate Ice Cream Superb: Follow recipe for Peach Ice Cream Superb. Omit peaches and lemon juice. Decrease sugar to 1¾ cups. Combine cream with **3 ounces (3 squares) unsweetened chocolate** in a saucepan and heat until chocolate is melted. Omit extracts. Stir in the sugar and salt until dissolved. Cool, then chill.

Apricot Ice Cream Superb: Follow recipe for Peach Ice Cream Superb. Substitute **1 pound (about 3 cups) dried apricots** for peaches. Put apricots into a saucepan with **4 cups water.** Cover and simmer 40 minutes, or until tender. Force apricots through a sieve or food mill. Decrease sugar to 1¾ cups and stir sugar and lemon juice into apricot pulp. Cool, then chill. Blend into cream mixture.

Vanilla Ice Cream Superb: Follow recipe for Peach Ice Cream Superb. Omit peaches, lemon juice, and almond extract. Decrease sugar to 1¼ cups. Increase vanilla extract to 3 tablespoons. Blend ingredients.

Strawberry Ice Cream Superb: Follow recipe for Peach Ice Cream Superb. Substitute 1½ **quarts fresh strawberries,** rinsed and hulled, for peaches. Force strawberries through a sieve or food mill, or purée in an electric blender. Combine crushed berries with sugar and lemon juice. Omit almond extract.

Tangerine Sherbet

1¼ **cups sugar**
2 **teaspoons grated tangerine peel**
½ **cup tangerine juice**
2 **tablespoons lemon juice**
⅛ **teaspoon salt**
2 **cups cream or half-and-half**
2 **or 3 drops orange food coloring**

1. Blend the ingredients in order in a bowl. Stir until sugar is dissolved. Pour into a refrigerator tray and freeze until mushy.
2. Turn mixture into a chilled bowl and beat with electric beater until smooth. Return mixture to tray and freeze until firm.

1½ pints sherbet

Grape Sherbet

2 envelopes unflavored gelatin
½ cup water
7 cups milk
4 cans (6 ounces each) frozen grape juice concentrate, thawed
1 tablespoon lemon juice
½ cup sugar

1. Soften gelatin in water in a saucepan. Dissolve over low heat, stirring constantly. Pour gelatin into a large bowl and stir in milk.
2. Blend in grape juice concentrate, lemon juice, and sugar. Mix thoroughly.
3. Pour into metal pans, not more than three quarters full. Place in freezer until mushy. Turn into a chilled bowl and beat until fluffy. Return to metal pans and freeze until firm.

About 1 gallon sherbet

Note: If desired, sherbet may be frozen in an ice cream freezer. Follow manufacturer's instructions, using ¼ cup rock salt to 1 quart crushed ice, chilling sherbet mixture thoroughly before churning. Sherbet may be kept frozen 2 to 3 weeks packed in a plastic container.

Hawaiian Sherbet: Substitute **4 cans (6 ounces each) frozen red fruit punch concentrate** for grape juice concentrate.

Orange Sherbet: Substitute **4 cans (6 ounces each) frozen orange juice concentrate** for grape juice concentrate. Increase sugar to 1½ to 2 cups, sweetening to taste.

Lemonade Sherbet: Substitute **4 cans (6 ounces each) frozen lemonade concentrate** for grape juice concentrate. Increase sugar to 2 to 2½ cups, sweetening to taste.

Boysenberry Ice

2 cans (16 ounces each) boysenberries, drained (reserve syrup)
2 tablespoons unflavored gelatin
¼ cup sugar
¾ cup water
1 tablespoon lemon juice

1. Force drained boysenberries through a fine sieve; set aside.
2. Mix gelatin and sugar in a saucepan. Stir in water and set over low heat until gelatin and sugar are dissolved, stirring constantly.
3. Remove from heat and stir in 1½ cups of the reserved syrup, boysenberries, and lemon juice.
4. Pour into a 1-quart refrigerator tray and freeze until firm, stirring several times.
5. Serve in chilled sherbet glasses.

About 1 quart ice

Strawberry Gelato

5 teaspoons unflavored gelatin
1½ cups sugar
4 cups milk
2 cups instant nonfat dry milk
2 packages (10 ounces each) frozen sliced strawberries, thawed
¼ cup kirsch
¼ teaspoon red food coloring

1. Thoroughly mix the gelatin and sugar in a large saucepan. Stir in the milk and then the nonfat dry milk. Stir over low heat until sugar and gelatin are dissolved. Set aside to cool.
2. Turn strawberries and kirsch into an electric blender container; add food coloring and blend until smooth. If necessary, strain through a fine sieve to remove seeds. Stir into cooled milk.
3. Pour into refrigerator trays and freeze until firm (2 to 3 hours.)
4. Spoon the amount of ice cream to be served into a bowl; allow it to soften slightly and whip until smooth, using an

*girls
dessert
in refrig
for after
class
Mom*

electric mixer. Spoon into chilled stemmed glasses and serve immediately.

About 2 quarts gelato

Strawberry-Banana Gelato: Follow recipe for Strawberry Gelato. Omit the frozen strawberries and kirsch. Combine **2 pints ripe strawberries,** rinsed, hulled, and crushed, with **¾ to 1 cup sugar** in a bowl. Mix and let stand about 1 hour. Turn half of the sweetened strawberries and **1 ripe banana,** peeled and cut in pieces, into an electric blender container; blend. Add remaining berries and blend thoroughly. Strain if necessary. Stir into cooled milk.

About 2½ quarts gelato

Mint Gelato: Follow recipe for Strawberry Gelato. Reduce gelatin to 4 teaspoons and sugar to 1 cup. Omit strawberries, kirsch, and food coloring. Stir **2 teaspoons vanilla extract** and **½ teaspoon mint extract** into cooled milk.

About 1½ quarts gelato

Pineapple-Orange-Buttermilk Sherbet

1 quart buttermilk
2 cups milk
2 cups sugar
2 cups fresh orange juice
1 can (8 ounces) crushed pineapple
    (undrained)
3 tablespoons fresh lemon juice
1 tablespoon vanilla extract

1. Combine buttermilk, milk, and sugar in a large bowl. Stir until sugar is dissolved.
2. Blend in orange juice, pineapple, lemon juice, and vanilla extract. (The mixture may appear curdled at this point.) Chill.
3. Pour mixture into refrigerator trays or metal pans, not more than three fourths full. Cover and freeze until mixture becomes firm around the edges.
4. Turn into a chilled bowl and beat or stir until smooth. Return to refrigerator trays and cover. Freeze until firm.
5. If not to be served soon after freezing, sherbet may be kept frozen in plastic containers 2 to 3 weeks.

About 1 gallon sherbet

Note: If desired, sherbet may be made in an ice cream freezer. Follow manufacturer's instructions and use ¼ cup rock salt to 1 quart crushed ice.

Grasshopper Sherbet

7 cups milk
1¼ cups sugar
¾ cup green crème de menthe
½ to ¾ cup white crème de cacao

1. Combine milk, sugar, crème de menthe, and crème de cacao in a large bowl. Stir until sugar is dissolved. Chill.
2. Pour mixture into refrigerator trays or metal pans, not more than three fourths full. Cover and freeze until mixture becomes firm around the edges.
3. Turn into a chilled bowl and beat or stir until smooth. Return to refrigerator trays and cover. Freeze until firm.
4. If not to be served soon after freezing, sherbet may be kept frozen in plastic containers 2 to 3 weeks.

About 3 quarts sherbet

Note: If desired, sherbet may be made in an ice cream freezer. Follow manufacturer's instructions and use ¼ cup rock salt to 1 quart crushed ice.

Lime Ice

2 teaspoons **unflavored gelatin**
2 cups **sugar**
3¼ cups **cold water**
¾ cup **lime juice**
2 tablespoons **lemon juice**
2 teaspoons **grated lemon peel**
Green food coloring

1. Mix gelatin and sugar in a saucepan. Stir in water and set over low heat until gelatin and sugar are dissolved, stirring constantly.
2. Blend in lime and lemon juices and lemon peel. Mix in food coloring, a drop at a time, to tint the desired color. Cool.
3. Pour into a refrigerator tray and freeze until firm, stirring several times.

1 quart ice

Apricot Ice: Follow recipe for Lime Ice. Decrease water to 1¾ cups and sugar to 1 cup. Substitute **2 cups apricot nectar** for lime juice and **orange juice** for lemon juice. Omit green food coloring.

Mocha Ice: Follow recipe for Lime Ice. Increase water to 3¾ cups. Decrease sugar to 1 cup. Mix **2 tablespoons instant coffee** with sugar and gelatin. Omit lime and lemon juices, lemon peel, and food coloring. Top with **sweetened whipped cream.**

Orange Ice: Follow recipe for Lime Ice. Decrease water to 2¼ cups and sugar to 1¼ cups. Substitute **2 cups orange juice** for lime juice and **orange peel** for lemon peel. Use **orange food coloring.**

Raspberry Ice: Follow recipe for Lime Ice. Decrease water to 2¼ cups and sugar to ¾ to 1 cup. Omit lime juice, lemon peel, and food coloring. Force **1 pint rinsed, sorted, and drained raspberries** through a fine sieve. Blend sieved raspberries into gelatin mixture with lemon juice.

Strawberry-Rhubarb Sherbet

3 cups **½-inch pieces fresh rhubarb**
3 cups **sliced fresh strawberries**
½ cup **sugar**
2 tablespoons **lemon juice**
6 cups **milk**
2 to 2½ cups **sugar**
¼ teaspoon **salt**

1. Combine rhubarb, 2 cups strawberries, and ½ cup sugar in a saucepan. Bring to boiling over medium heat, stirring frequently. Boil until rhubarb is tender (about 2 minutes).
2. Stir in remaining 1 cup strawberries. Purée in a blender or put through a food mill. Cool. Add lemon juice.
3. Combine the fruit purée, milk, 2 to 2½ cups sugar, and salt in a large bowl. Mix thoroughly. Pour into a metal pan, no more than three quarters full. Freeze until mushy. Turn into a chilled bowl and beat until fluffy. Return to metal pan. Freeze until firm.

3 to 4 quarts sherbet

Note: If desired, sherbet may be frozen in an ice cream freezer. Follow manufacturer's instructions, using ¼ cup rock salt to 1 quart crushed ice, chilling sherbet mixture thoroughly before churning. Sherbet may be kept frozen 2 to 3 weeks packed in a plastic container.

Strawberry Sherbet: Follow recipe for Strawberry-Rhubarb Sherbet. Use **6 cups strawberries** and omit rhubarb.

Tropical Ice

1⅓ cups sugar
1⅓ cups water
½ cup lemon juice
2 ripe bananas, peeled and cut in pieces
¼ cup lightly packed brown sugar
3½ cups unsweetened pineapple juice
½ cup orange juice

1. Combine sugar and water in a saucepan. Heat, stirring until sugar is dissolved. Cover and bring to boiling; boil about 5 minutes. Set the syrup aside to cool.
2. Put lemon juice, banana, and brown sugar into an electric blender container. Blend until smooth. Gradually add the pineapple and orange juices and blend thoroughly. Mix with the sugar syrup.
3. Turn into refrigerator trays and freeze, stirring the mixture occasionally, until firm.
4. Spoon ice into serving dishes.

About 1½ pints ice

Baked Alaska

1 quart chocolate ice cream
1 quart strawberry ice cream
Pound cake, sponge cake, or ladyfingers
5 egg whites
½ teaspoon vanilla extract
¼ teaspoon salt
¾ cup sugar

1. Line a chilled 2-quart melon mold with chocolate ice cream. Pack firmly against sides of mold. Fill center of mold with strawberry ice cream, packing firmly. Freeze until firm.
2. Cut a layer of cake about ¼ inch larger than mold and about 1¼ inches thick. Place on a wooden board or on a baking sheet lined with 2 sheets of heavy paper; set aside.
3. Beat egg whites with vanilla extract and salt until frothy; gradually add sugar, beating constantly until stiff peaks are formed.
4. Unmold ice cream onto center of cake. Working quickly, completely cover ice cream and cake with meringue, spreading evenly and being careful to completely seal bottom edge. With spatula, quickly swirl meringue into an attractive design and, if desired, garnish with maraschino cherries.
5. Set in a 450°F oven 4 to 5 minutes, or until meringue is lightly browned. Quickly slide onto a chilled serving place, slice and serve immediately. (If not ready to serve immediately, place baked Alaska in freezer so ice cream does not melt.)

12 to 16 servings

Note: If desired, a layer of fresh fruit (orange, mandarin orange, or grapefruit sections, sliced peaches, etc.) may be arranged over cake slice before unmolding ice cream over it.

Baked Alaska Loaf: Follow recipe for Baked Alaska. Substitute **1-quart brick ice cream** for molded ice cream. Cut cake about ¼ inch larger than mold on all sides.

Individual Baked Alaskas: Follow the recipe for Baked Alaska. Decrease ice cream to 1½ pints chocolate, strawberry, or vanilla. Omit cake. Chill **8 canned pineapple slices.** Pat dry with absorbent paper and arrange on a thick wooden board. Quickly place 1 scoop of very firm ice cream in center of each slice. Completely cover ice cream with meringue, spreading evenly. Be careful to completely seal bottom edge to pineapple slice. Set in a 450°F oven about 4 minutes, or until meringue is lightly browned. Serve immediately. (Place in freezer if not ready to serve immediately.)

8 servings

Wheat-Germ Ice Cream Bars with Peach Sauce

1 cup toasted wheat germ
2 tablespoons sugar
¼ teaspoon ground cinnamon
2 tablespoons butter or margarine, melted
2 pint bricks vanilla ice cream
Peach Sauce

1. For ice cream bars, combine wheat germ, sugar, cinnamon, and butter.
2. Cut each pint of ice cream in thirds crosswise. Roll each piece in wheat-germ mixture to coat and put onto a chilled tray. Store in freezer until ready to serve.
3. Prepare Peach Sauce.
4. To serve, spoon Peach Sauce over ice cream bars.

6 servings

Peach Sauce: Combine ½ cup sugar, 2 tablespoons cornstarch, ¼ teaspoon ground cinnamon, and ¼ teaspoon ground nutmeg in a saucepan; mix well. Add 1 package (10 ounces) frozen sliced peaches, thawed; stir. Bring to boiling, stirring until sauce is thickened. Cool.

About 1¾ cups sauce

Frozen Cherry Easter Egg

3 pints vanilla ice cream, softened
1½ cups chopped candied red cherries
¾ cup chopped toasted filberts
¼ cup finely chopped flaked coconut
3 tablespoons maraschino cherry syrup
1 tablespoon vanilla extract
1 package (1½ ounces) dessert topping mix, prepared according to package directions

1. Mix into softened ice cream the cherries, filberts, and coconut, then a blend of the syrup and vanilla extract. Pack mixture into a 1½-quart melon mold, which has been rinsed with cold water and drained. Cover and freeze until firm (about 3 hours).
2. Invert the mold on a chilled plate. Dip a clean towel in hot water, quickly wring it almost dry, and wrap it around the mold for a few seconds; lift off mold. If mold cannot be lifted off immediately, repeat. If necessary, set in freezer before frosting.
3. Frost the egg with the whipped dessert topping. Decorate, using a cake decorating set (aerosol cans of tinted frosting with decorating tips) or your favorite decorating frosting and pastry bag with decorating tubes. Pipe frosting onto frozen egg in an attractive design. Garnish with whole **candied red cherries.** Set in freezer until ready to serve.

10 to 12 servings

Low Calorie Desserts

Baked Apples

6 medium-size firm apples (about 2 pounds)
¾ teaspoon cinnamon
½ teaspoon nutmeg
½ cup sugar
½ cup water
Few drops red food coloring

1. Wash the apples and remove cores with an apple corer. Pare about a 1-inch strip at stem end. Set apples, pared end up, in a 2-quart casserole.
2. Mix cinnamon and nutmeg. Sprinkle in centers of apples.
3. Mix sugar, water, and food coloring in a saucepan and bring just to boiling. Pour syrup over apples. Cover casserole.
4. Bake at 350°F 45 to 50 minutes, or until apples are tender, basting every 5 minutes for first 15 minutes, then every 15 minutes.
5. Serve warm or cold.

6 servings

Baked Pears: Follow recipe for Baked Apples; substitute **3 large pears** for apples. Cut in half and core. Bake at 350°F 35 to 40 minutes.

Orange Molds

1 envelope unflavored gelatin
¾ cup cold water
¼ cup sugar
1 can (6 ounces) frozen orange juice concentrate
½ cup ice water
Lemon slices or fresh mint sprigs

1. Sprinkle gelatin over cold water in a saucepan. Stir constantly over low heat until gelatin dissolves (about 3 minutes). Remove from heat.
2. Add sugar, stirring until dissolved. Add frozen orange juice concentrate and stir until it is melted and blended. Stir in ice water.
3. Pour gelatin mixture into 4 individual molds. Chill until firm. Unmold in dessert dishes. If desired, garnish with mint sprigs.

4 servings

Nectarine Whip

4 fully ripe nectarines, peeled and
  pitted
  Lime juice
  Vanilla extract
2 cups whipped dessert topping, or
  frozen dessert topping, thawed

1. Add quartered nectarines to the container of an electric blender. Using the electric blender according to manufacturer's directions, blend only until partially smooth (should make 2 cups; do not liquefy). Drizzle pulp with a little lime juice and a few drops of the vanilla extract.
2. Fold pulp into topping and chill thoroughly.
3. To serve, pile into chilled stemmed sherbet glasses. If desired, garnish each with nectarine slices and **mint sprigs.**

8 servings

Spiced Strawberries

½ cup sugar
½ cup water
2 cinnamon sticks
5 whole cloves
½ cup orange juice
¼ cup lemon juice
2 pints fresh strawberries, sliced

1. Combine sugar, water, cinnamon, and cloves in a saucepan. Heat to boiling. Cook over low heat 5 minutes.
2. Remove from heat. Add orange and lemon juices. Cool. Discard spices. Add strawberries. Chill about 2 hours, stirring occasionally.

6 servings

Raspberry Freeze

1 egg, separated
½ cup instant nonfat dry milk
⅓ cup water
⅓ cup sugar
3 tablespoons lemon juice
1 package (10 ounces) frozen
  raspberries, thawed (do not
  drain)

1. Combine egg white, dry milk, and water in a bowl; beat until fluffy. Add sugar and lemon juice gradually, beating until mixture is stiff. Beat in egg yolk until mixed. Fold in raspberries.
2. Turn mixture into a 1-quart refrigerator tray and freeze until firm.

About 1 quart sherbet

Note: Frozen strawberries, peaches, or cherries may be substituted for the raspberries.

Elegant Champagne Ice

¾ cup sugar
1½ cups water
1 medium lemon
2 medium oranges
3 tablespoons orange liqueur
3 cups champagne
2½ cups fresh strawberries
¼ to ⅓ cup sugar

1. Combine ¾ cup sugar and water in a saucepan. Bring to boiling and cook 5 minutes; cool.
2. Using a vegetable peeler or paring knife, remove peel from lemon and 1 orange. Add the peels to the cooled syrup with the orange liqueur. Chill the syrup 2 hours; remove peels.
3. Squeeze the juice from the lemon and oranges. Stir into the chilled mixture with 2 cups champagne. Freeze until mushy. Beat with a rotary beater until smooth, and place in an 11×7-inch metal pan. Freeze several hours, stirring occasionally.
4. While ice is freezing, clean and hull the strawberries. Halve the berries, reserving 6 to 8 whole strawberries. Sprinkle ¼ to ⅓ cup sugar over strawberry halves and pour in remaining champagne. Refrigerate 4 hours.
5. When ready to serve, place strawberries in sherbet glasses, fill with champagne ice, and top with a whole berry.

6 to 8 servings

Citrus-Ginger Sherbet

½ cup water
1½ cups sugar
4 egg whites
3 cups ginger ale
1 cup orange juice
½ cup lemon juice
½ cup pineapple juice
Lime slices (optional)

1. Combine water with 1 cup sugar in a saucepan. Heat to boiling and cook until syrup reaches 234° to 238°F (softball stage).
2. Beat egg whites until stiff. Continue beating while gradually adding remaining sugar. Slowly pour the hot syrup into the egg whites, beating constantly until mixture cools.
3. Gradually beat in ginger ale and fruit juices. Place in the freezer until partially frozen; remove and whip quickly. Pour into a 10×10×2-inch metal pan, cover, and freeze until firm.
4. Spoon into individual serving dishes and, if desired, top with a slice of lime.

8 to 10 servings

Ambrosia

3 medium oranges
Sugar
⅔ cup shredded or flaked coconut, coarsely chopped

1. Peel the oranges, cut away white membrane, and remove sections; or cut into thin crosswise slices, removing any seeds, and cut slices in halves.
2. Arrange orange sections in several layers in a serving bowl, sprinkling each layer of oranges with sugar and coconut.
3. Chill at least 1 hour.

4 servings

Banana Ambrosia: Peel **2 ripe bananas** and slice about ¼ inch thick. Alternate layers of orange, coconut, and banana in bowl, ending with orange. Just before serving, garnish with additional banana slices, if desired.

Pineapple Ambrosia: Follow recipe for Ambrosia. Substitute about **¾ cup diced fresh pineapple** or **drained pineapple chunks** for 1 of the oranges.

Strawberry Ambrosia: Follow recipe for Ambrosia. Reduce oranges to 2 and coconut to ½ cup. Omit sugar. Layer oranges and coconut with contents of **1 package (10 ounces) frozen sliced strawberries,** thawed. Chill 30 minutes.

Honey-Walnut Fruit Dessert

½ small ripe pineapple
2 oranges
1 red apple, diced
1 medium cucumber, pared and diced
1 tablespoon lemon juice
½ cup honey
¼ cup chopped walnuts
2 tablespoons lemon juice

1. Remove all fruit from pineapple shell. Core and dice fruit. Peel the oranges, section, and cut into pieces.
2. Combine orange pieces, pineapple, apple, and cucumber in a bowl. Add 1 tablespoon lemon juice and mix well. Chill.
3. Meanwhile, combine honey, walnuts, and 2 tablespoons lemon juice in a small saucepan. Heat, stirring to blend. Cool; chill.
4. When ready to serve, drain fruit mixture and spoon into dessert dishes. Spoon some honey-walnut mixture over each serving.

About 6 servings

Filled Nut Torte

4 egg whites
¾ cup sugar
4 egg yolks
1 cup fine, dry bread crumbs
1 teaspoon baking powder
¾ cup ground walnuts
Filling
Confectioners' sugar

1. Grease bottoms of two 8-inch round layer cake pans; line bottoms with waxed paper. Set aside.
2. Beat egg whites until stiff peaks are formed. Gradually add ½ cup sugar, beating until stiff; set aside.
3. Beat egg yolks, gradually adding remaining ¼ cup sugar, until they are very thick and lemon-colored. Combine bread crumbs and baking powder. Blend into egg yolks with nuts. Fold in beaten egg whites. Turn batter into prepared pans.
4. Bake at 375°F 20 minutes, or until done. Cool in pans on wire racks 5 minutes. Remove from pans, peel off waxed paper, and cool completely on wire racks.
5. Spread top of 1 layer with desired filling. Place other layer on top and sift confectioners' sugar over torte.

12 servings

Fillings: Use ¾ cup canned whole cranberry sauce; 1 cup prepared packaged vanilla instant pudding made with ¾ cup liquefied nonfat dry milk; or ⅓ cup semisweet chocolate pieces, melted with 2 tablespoons liquefied nonfat dry milk (or skim milk) over hot, not boiling, water.

Sea-Foam Frosted Cupcakes

Cupcakes:
½ cup sifted cake flour
½ teaspoon baking powder
⅛ teaspoon salt
1 egg
3 tablespoons sugar
¾ teaspoon lemon juice
2½ tablespoons hot nonfat dry milk
   or skim milk

Frosting:
¼ cup light corn syrup
1 egg white
Dash salt
½ teaspoon vanilla extract
Food coloring (optional)
Multicolored nonpareilles or
   grated lemon peel

1. To make cupcakes, sift flour with baking powder and salt 3 times; set aside.
2. Beat egg until very thick and light (about 5 minutes). Gradually add sugar, beating constantly. Beat in lemon juice.
3. Fold in flour mixture, a small amount at a time. Add hot milk and stir quickly to blend. Immediately pour batter into 8 lightly greased 2½-inch muffin pan wells.
4. Bake at 350°F 12 to 15 minutes, or until a wooden pick inserted in center comes out clean. Cool in pan 10 minutes. Remove to wire rack and cool completely.
5. To make frosting, bring the syrup to boiling in a small saucepan. Beat egg white with salt until stiff but not dry. Slowly add the hot syrup, beating until mixture forms rounded peaks. Add vanilla extract. If desired, tint frosting before spreading on cooled cupcakes. Sprinkle nonpareilles on frosted cupcakes.

8 cupcakes

Pastries, Pies, and Tarts

Cream Puff or Choux Paste

1 cup hot water
½ cup butter
1 tablespoon sugar
½ teaspoon salt
1 cup all-purpose flour
4 eggs

1. Put hot water, butter, sugar, and salt into a saucepan and bring to a rolling boil.
2. Add the flour all at one time. Beat vigorously with a wooden spoon until mixture leaves sides of pan and forms a smooth ball. Remove from heat.
3. Add eggs, one at a time, beating until mixture is smooth after each addition. Continue beating until mixture is thick and smooth.
4. Dough may be used immediately or may be wrapped in waxed paper and refrigerated overnight.

French Pastry Cream (Crème Pâtisserie)

3 tablespoons flour
6 tablespoons sugar
¼ teaspoon salt
½ cup cold milk
1½ cups milk, scalded
4 egg yolks, slightly beaten
1 teaspoon vanilla extract

1. Thoroughly blend flour, sugar, and salt in the top of a double boiler. Add the cold milk, stirring well. Gradually. stir in scalded milk. Bring to boiling over direct heat, stirring constantly; cook 2 minutes.
2. Set over boiling water. Vigorously stir about 3 tablespoons of hot mixture into egg yolks. Immediately blend into mixture in double boiler. Cook over simmering water 3 to 5 minutes; stir slowly to keep mixture cooking evenly.
3. Remove from heat and strain into a bowl. Stir in vanilla extract. Cover and cool. Chill.

About 2 cups pastry cream

Cream Puffs

Cream Puff or Choux Paste (page 57)
French Pastry Cream (page 57)
Confectioners' sugar

1. Force puff paste dough through a pastry tube or drop by tablespoonfuls 2 inches apart onto a lightly greased baking sheet.
2. Bake at 450°F 15 minutes. Turn oven control to 350°F and bake 20 to 25 minutes longer, or until golden brown. Remove to rack and cool.
3. Cut off tops of puffs and pull out any soft, moist dough. Fill with French Pastry Cream. Replace tops and sift confectioners' sugar over cream puffs.

1 dozen large cream puffs

Miniature Puffs: Follow recipe for Cream Puffs. Drop dough by teaspoonfuls onto lightly greased baking sheets. Bake at 450°F 10 minutes. Turn oven control to 350°F and bake 5 minutes longer, or until golden brown. Complete as directed for large cream puffs.

4 dozen miniature cream puffs

Éclairs

Cream Puff or Choux Paste (page 57)
French Pastry Cream (page 57)
1 ounce (1 square) unsweetened chocolate
¾ cup confectioners' sugar
1 teaspoon dark corn syrup
1 tablespoon cream
2 teaspoons boiling water
1 teaspoon butter
½ teaspoon vanilla extract

1. Form cream puff paste into 4½×1-inch oblongs, about 2 inches apart on a lightly greased baking sheet.
2. Bake at 450°F 15 minutes. Turn oven control to 350°F and bake 20 to 25 minutes longer, or until golden brown. Remove to a rack to cool.
3. Cut a slit in the side of éclair and pull out any soft, moist dough. Force French Pastry Cream into éclair.
4. Melt chocolate in a heavy saucepan and add confectioners' sugar, corn syrup, cream, water, and butter. Place over low heat and stir constantly until butter melts. Remove from heat and stir in vanilla extract. Cool slightly and spread evenly over tops of éclairs.

1 dozen éclairs

Napoleons

Pastry:
1 cup butter
2 cups sifted all-purpose flour
½ teaspoon salt
7 tablespoons water

Filling:
⅓ pound (about 1 cup) blanched almonds, finely ground
½ cup confectioners' sugar
3 tablespoons butter
2 egg yolks
1 tablespoon rum or kirsch
Napoleon Glaze
Decorating Chocolate

1. To make pastry, put butter into a large bowl of cold water and ice cubes or chipped ice. Work butter with hands. Break it into small portions and squeeze each in water about 20 times, or until butter is pliable and waxy. Remove and wipe off excess water. Reserve ¼ cup of this butter. Pat remainder ½ inch thick, divide into 5 equal portions, wrap each in waxed paper. Chill in refrigerator until firm.
2. Sift flour and salt together into a bowl. With pastry blender or two knives, cut in the ¼ cup butter until pieces are the size of small peas. Add water gradually, stir in with a fork. When blended, gather into a ball and knead on lightly floured surface until elastic and smooth. Cover with bowl and let ripen about 30 minutes.
3. Roll on a floured surface to form a rectangle ¼ inch thick. Keep corners square, gently pulling dough into shape where necessary. Remove one portion of chilled butter and cut into

small pieces. Quickly pat pieces down center third of dough. Cover butter with right-hand third of dough. Fold left-hand third under butter section. With rolling pin gently press down and seal the open edges. Wrap pastry in waxed paper. Chill in refrigerator about 1 hour.

4. Remove from refrigerator and place on the floured surface with butter section near top, narrow width toward you. Turn folded dough one-quarter way around, to have open edge away from you. Roll to original size. Repeat four times the procedure for folding, sealing, and chilling, using second third, fourth, and fifth portions of butter. Each time place dough on floured surface, turn, and roll as directed.

5. With last rolling, fold four sides toward center. Gently press down with rolling pin. Fold in half. Wrap dough in waxed paper. Cover with a damp towel. Chill in refrigerator about 2 hours. (Dough may be stored several days, wrapped in waxed paper in refrigerator.)

6. Divide pastry into thirds. Immediately return two portions to refrigerator. Roll remaining portion into a 12×10-inch rectangle about ⅛ inch thick. Cut into 8 even 3×5-inch strips. Trim ends so all strips are equal.

7. Transfer to baking sheet rinsed with cold water and drained thoroughly. Prick well. Repeat process with each remaining portion of pastry. Chill in refrigerator 30 minutes.

8. Bake at 425°F 10 minutes; turn oven control to 325°F and bake 20 minutes, or until golden brown. Remove to racks.

9. When cold, split each slice lengthwise. Let stand about 30 minutes to dry.

10. To make filling, mix the almonds with the confectioners' sugar. Cream the butter until softened. Beat in the egg yolks, one at a time, then the rum. Continue beating until blended. Mix in the almond-sugar mixture.

11. To assemble Napoleons, fill one split slice with some of the almond filling. Gently press together. Spread more filling over top and cover with one half of another slice, cut-side down. Spread top with more filling and cover with remaining half of slice. This completes one Napoleon, excepting the glaze.

12. Spread glaze on tops of Napoleons. Pipe the Decorating Chocolate in parallel lines across the width of each cake; draw a wooden pick lengthwise across chocolate lines before chocolate sets.

1 dozen Napoleons

Napoleon Glaze: Mix in a heavy saucepan ¾ **cup confectioners' sugar, 1 tablespoon hot water, 1 teaspoon light corn syrup,** and **2 teaspoons butter.** Place over low heat, stirring constantly until butter melts. Add ½ **teaspoon vanilla extract.** Use immediately.

Decorating Chocolate: Melt **semisweet chocolate** over hot (not simmering) water, then cool it enough so it can be piped through a decorating tube. If chocolate is too thin, stir in a small amount of **confectioners' sugar.**

Strudel

4 cups sifted all-purpose flour
1 egg, fork beaten
1 tablespoon melted butter
1 tablespoon cider vinegar
    Lukewarm water (80° to 85°F)
    Melted butter
    Flour
    Melted butter
    Fine dry bread crumbs
    Strudel Fillings
    Egg, fork beaten

1. Put flour into a large bowl and make a well in center; add egg and butter. Put vinegar into a measuring cup and fill with lukewarm water to make 1 cup. Gradually add to ingredients in bowl, mixing until all flour is moistened.
2. Turn dough onto a lightly floured pastry board and knead. Hold dough high above board and hit it hard against the board 100 to 125 times, or until dough is smooth and elastic and small bubbles appear on the surface. Knead dough occasionally during the hitting process. Shape dough into a smooth round ball and put onto a lightly floured board. Lightly brush top of dough with melted butter. Cover dough with an inverted bowl and allow to rest 30 minutes.
3. Cover a table (about 48×30 inches) with a clean cloth and sprinkle the cloth evenly with ½ cup flour.
4. Place dough on center of cloth and sprinkle very lightly with flour. Roll dough into a rectangle ¼ to ⅛ inch thick.
5. Clench the fists, tucking the thumbs under the fingers. With the palm-side of fists down, reach under the dough to its center (dough will rest on back of hands). Being careful not to tear dough, stretch the center of the dough gently and steadily toward you as you slowly walk around the table. (Dough should not have any torn spots, if possible, but such perfection will come with practice.)
6. As the center becomes as thin as paper, concentrate the stretching motion closer to the edge of the dough. Continue until dough is as thin as tissue paper and hangs over edge of table. With kitchen shears, trim edges, leaving about 2 inches of dough overhanging on all sides.
7. Allow stretched dough to dry about 5 minutes, or until it is no longer sticky. Avoid drying dough too long since it will become brittle.
8. Sprinkle melted butter and bread crumbs over dough. Cover dough with one of the Strudel Fillings.
9. Fold the overhanging dough on all sides over the filling, making strudel even with edge of table. Beginning at one narrow end of table, grasp the cloth with both hands; slowly lift cloth and fold over a strip of dough about 3 inches wide. Pull cloth toward you; again lift cloth and slowly and loosely roll dough, making roll about 3 inches wide. Brush off excess flour from the roll; cut roll into halves and place in a buttered 15×10-inch jelly-roll pan. Brush top and sides with fork-beaten egg.
10. Bake at 350°F about 40 minutes, or until strudel is golden brown. Remove to wire rack. Sift **confectioners' sugar** over top of strudel. Cut into 2½-inch slices and serve warm or cooled.

1 dozen slices

STRUDEL FILLINGS

Cherry Filling: Drain **2 cans (17 ounces each) pitted tart red cherries.** Put cherries between layers of absorbent paper and pat gently to remove any excess liquid. Mix **¾ cup chopped toasted blanched almonds, 1 cup sugar,** and **½ teaspoon ground cinnamon.** Sprinkle prepared strudel dough with cherries and almond mixture.

Poppy Seed Filling: Mix ½ **pound freshly ground poppy seed, 1 cup sugar, ½ cup raisins,** and **2 teaspoons grated lemon peel** and spoon over prepared strudel dough.

Apple and Currant Filling: Core and pare 1½ **pounds tart apples.** Cut apples into ⅛-inch slices. Spoon apple slices and ½ **cup currants** or **raisins** over prepared strudel dough. Sprinkle with a mixture of ¾ **cup sugar, 1 teaspoon ground cinnamon, ⅛ teaspoon nutmeg,** and **1 teaspoon grated lemon** or **orange peel.**

Cottage Cheese Filling: Beat **2 egg yolks, ¼ cup sugar,** and **¼ teaspoon salt** until thick. Add **1 pound dry cottage cheese** gradually to egg mixture, beating well. Stir in ¼ **cup raisins, ½ teaspoon vanilla extract,** and ½ **teaspoon grated lemon peel.** Spoon filling in small mounds on prepared strudel dough and spread evenly.

Dried Fruit Filling: Mix **1 cup finely chopped dried apricots, 1 cup finely chopped prunes, 1 teaspoon grated orange peel, 2 tablespoons orange juice, ½ cup sugar,** and **2 table-spoons honey,** warmed. Spread over prepared strudel dough. Sprinkle with ½ **teaspoon ground nutmeg.**

Chopped Nut Filling: Mix ½ **pound blanched al-monds,** finely ground, **4 egg yolks, ½ cup sugar,** and **1 teaspoon grated lemon peel** to form a paste. Spread in rows on prepared strudel dough. Drizzle with ¼ **cup melted butter.**

Raisin and Cherry Filling: Mix **4 cups ground rai-sins, 1 jar (8 ounces) maraschino cherries, 4 cups chopped filberts, 2 cups sugar, 2 cups ground bread or cake crumbs,** and ¼ **cup lemon juice.** Place on prepared strudel dough in rows fairly close together. Cut **Turkish paste** into small cubes and wedge into rows every few inches. (Or use **orange marmalade** and drop half teaspoonfuls into rows.)

Jelly Filling: Sprinkle prepared strudel dough generous-ly with **cinnamon** and **sugar.** Mix ¾ **cup chopped nuts, 1 cup golden raisins, 1 pint cherry, plum,** or **watermelon preserves, 1 cup fine bread crumbs,** and **1 teaspoon grated lemon peel.** Place a row of filling on dough every few inches.

Marlborough Pie

1½ cups applesauce
¾ cup firmly packed brown sugar
4 eggs, slightly beaten
¼ cup butter or margarine, melted
1 teaspoon grated lemon peel
3 tablespoons lemon juice
½ teaspoon salt
¼ teaspoon ground nutmeg
1 unbaked 9-inch pastry shell (page 62)

1. Combine applesauce, brown sugar, eggs, butter, lemon peel and juice, salt, and nutmeg; mix well. Turn into pastry shell.
2. Bake at 450°F 15 minutes. Turn oven control to 300°F and bake 45 to 55 minutes, or until a knife comes out clean when inserted in filling halfway between center and edge. Cool on a wire rack.

One 9-inch pie

Spicy Pear Dumplings

2¾ cups all-purpose flour
1 tablespoon sugar
½ teaspoon salt
¾ cup lard
½ to ⅔ cup cold water
6 fresh Anjou pears, pared and cored (reserve peelings)
1½ cups lightly packed brown sugar
½ teaspoon ground mace, ground coriander, or anise seed, crushed
2 tablespoons butter or margarine
1 cup water
1 teaspoon cornstarch
⅛ teaspoon salt
1 tablespoon lemon juice
1 tablespoon butter or margarine

1. Combine flour, sugar, and salt in a bowl. Cut in lard with a pastry blender or two knives until pieces are the size of small peas. Sprinkle enough water over mixture, about 1 tablespoon at a time, mixing lightly with a fork after each addition until dough can be easily gathered into a ball.
2. Divide dough into halves and shape each into a ball. Roll each into a round about 14 inches in diameter. Using a pastry wheel, divide each round into 3 equal wedge-shaped pieces. Place one pear in the center of each portion and spoon about 1 tablespoon of a mixture of brown sugar and spice into each pear cavity. Dot pears with the 2 tablespoons butter. Fold pastry up over pears, moistening edges to seal. Place the dumplings in buttered individual ramekins; set aside.
3. Combine pear peelings and water in a saucepan; bring to boiling and simmer, covered, about 5 minutes. Strain, discarding peelings, and add enough water to make 1 cup liquid.
4. Combine remaining brown sugar mixture, cornstarch, and salt. Stir in pear liquid, lemon juice, and butter. Bring to boiling and boil about 3 minutes. Pour syrup equally over pears in ramekins; cover each closely with aluminum foil.
5. Bake at 425°F 10 minutes; turn oven control to 375°F and continue baking about 30 minutes, or until pastry is golden brown and pears are tender. Uncover last 20 minutes of baking.
6. Serve pears warm, spooning some of the sauce in the bottom of the ramekins over them. Accompany with **cream.**

6 servings

Pastry for 1-Crust Pie

1 cup all-purpose flour
½ teaspoon salt
⅓ cup lard or vegetable shortening
2 to 3 tablespoons cold water

1. Sift flour and salt together into a bowl. Cut in shortening with pastry blender or two knives until pieces are the size of small peas.
2. Sprinkle the water over mixture, a teaspoonful at a time, mixing lightly with a fork after each addition. Add only enough water to hold pastry together. Work quickly; do not overhandle. Shape into a ball and flatten on a lightly floured surface.
3. Roll from center to edge into a round about ⅛ inch thick and about 1 inch larger than overall size of pan.
4. Loosen pastry from surface with spatula and fold in quarters. Gently lay pastry in pan and unfold it, fitting it to pan so it is not stretched.
5. Trim edge with scissors or sharp knife so pastry extends about ½ inch beyond edge of pie pan. Fold extra pastry under at edge, and flute.
6. Thoroughly prick bottom and sides of shell with a fork. (Omit pricking if filling is to be baked in shell.)
7. Bake at 450°F 10 to 15 minutes, or until crust is light golden brown.
8. Cool on rack.

One 8- or 9-inch pie shell

Pastry for 2-Crust Pie: Double the recipe for Pastry for 1-Crust Pie. Divide pastry into halves and shape into a ball. Roll each ball as in Pastry for 1-Crust Pie. For top crust, roll out one ball of pastry and cut 1 inch larger than pie pan. Slit pastry with knife in several places to allow steam to escape during baking. Gently fold in half and set aside while rolling bottom crust. Roll second ball of pastry and gently fit pastry into pie pan; avoid stretching. Trim pastry with scissors or sharp knife around edge of pan. Do not prick. Fill as directed in specific recipe. Moisten edge with water for a tight seal. Carefully arrange top crust over filling. Gently press edges to seal. Fold extra pastry under bottom pastry, and flute edge.

Cheese Pastry for 2-Crust Pie: Follow recipe for Pastry for 2-Crust Pie. Cut in **1 cup (4 ounces) finely shredded Cheddar cheese** with the lard or shortening.

Fresh Lemon Meringue Pie

Filling:
  1½ cups sugar
  6 tablespoons cornstarch
  ¼ teaspoon salt
  ½ cup cold water
  ½ cup fresh lemon juice
  3 egg yolks, well beaten
  2 tablespoons butter or margarine
  1½ cups boiling water
  1 teaspoon freshly grated lemon
       peel
  1 baked 9-inch pastry shell (page
       62)

Meringue:
  3 egg whites (at room temperature)
  ¼ teaspoon cream of tartar
  6 tablespoons sugar

1. For filling, mix sugar, cornstarch, and salt together in a 2- to 3-quart saucepan. Using a wire whisk, gradually blend in cold water, then lemon juice, until smooth. Add egg yolks, blending very thoroughly. Add butter. Slowly add boiling water, stirring constantly with a rubber spatula.
2. Over medium to high heat, gradually bring mixture to a full boil, stirring gently and constantly with spatula. Reduce heat slightly as mixture begins to thicken. Boil gently 1 minute. Remove from heat and stir in lemon peel.
3. Pour hot filling into pastry shell. Let stand, allowing a thin film to form while preparing meringue.
4. For meringue, beat egg whites with an electric mixer several seconds until frothy. Add cream of tartar and beat on high speed until egg whites have just lost their foamy appearance. They should bend over slightly when beaters are withdrawn, forming soft peaks.
5. Reduce speed to medium while gradually adding sugar, about 1 tablespoon at a time. Return to high speed and beat until egg whites are fairly stiff, but still glossy. Soft peaks should be formed when beaters are withdrawn.
6. Place meringue on hot filling in several mounds around edge of pie. Push meringue to edge of crust to seal. Cover rest of filling by gently pushing meringue towards center of pie.
7. Bake at 350°F 12 to 15 minutes, or until golden brown. Cool on a wire rack at room temperature away from drafts for 2 hours before cutting and serving.

One 9-inch pie

Lime Chiffon Pie

1 envelope unflavored gelatin
¼ cup cold water
4 egg yolks, slightly beaten
⅔ cup sugar
2 teaspoons grated lime peel
½ cup lime juice
¼ teaspoon salt
2 to 3 drops green food coloring
4 egg whites
½ cup sugar
1 baked 9-inch pastry shell (page 62)
Whipped cream

1. Soften gelatin in cold water; set aside.
2. Mix the egg yolks, sugar, lime peel and juice, and salt together in top of a double boiler. Cook over simmering water, stirring constantly, until mixture is slightly thickened.
3. Remove from water and blend in gelatin, stirring until gelatin is dissolved. Mix in the food coloring. Cool. Chill until mixture is partially set.
4. Beat egg whites until frothy; gradually add ½ cup sugar, beating constantly until stiff peaks are formed. Spread over gelatin mixture and fold together. Turn into pastry shell. Chill until firm.
5. Garnish wedges of pie with whipped cream and serve.

One 9-inch pie

Lemon Chiffon Pie: Follow recipe for Lime Chiffon Pie. Substitute **lemon peel and juice** for lime peel and juice. Substitute **yellow food coloring** for green.

Dakkeri Chiffon Pie: Follow recipe for Lime Chiffon Pie. Use an 8-inch pie pan. Decrease egg yolks and egg whites to 3. Blend ⅓ **cup light rum** into cooled gelatin mixture. Garnish with thin slices of **lime**.

Orange Chiffon Pie: Follow recipe for Lime Chiffon Pie. Substitute **2 tablespoons lemon juice** for 2 tablespoons of the water. Substitute **orange peel and juice** for lime peel and juice. Omit food coloring.

Swiss Apple Pie

6 tablespoons butter
1½ cups all-purpose flour
3 to 4 tablespoons cold water
1 tablespoon ground toasted almonds
1 tablespoon fine dry bread crumbs
1½ pounds tart apples, pared and thinly sliced
2 eggs
2 egg yolks
2 cups whipping cream
½ cup sugar
2 tablespoons butter, melted
¼ cup sugar

1. Cut butter into flour with a pastry blender or two knives until the pieces are size of small peas. Add water gradually, mixing with a fork until pastry holds together. Shape into a ball.
2. Roll pastry about ⅛ inch thick on a lightly floured surface. Line a 10-inch pie pan with pastry; flute edge. Sprinkle a mixture of almonds and crumbs over bottom; cover with apples.
3. Bake at 350°F 5 minutes.
4. Meanwhile, beat eggs and egg yolks slightly; add cream and ½ cup sugar; blend well. Pour half of the mixture over the apples.
5. Bake until firm (about 30 minutes). Pour remaining mixture over apples and continue baking about 45 minutes, or until a metal knife inserted halfway between center and edge of pie comes out clean.
6. Remove pie from oven and pour melted butter evenly over top. Sprinkle with remaining sugar and return to oven for 5 minutes. Cool before serving.

One 10-inch pie

Cherry-Berry-Peach Pie, 66

Pumpkin-Crunch Chiffon Pie

½ cup crunchy peanut butter
1 baked 9-inch pastry shell (page 62)
1 envelope unflavored gelatin
¼ cup cold water
1½ cups canned pumpkin
½ cup sugar
½ cup milk
3 egg yolks, well beaten
½ teaspoon each ginger, nutmeg, and cinnamon
¼ teaspoon salt
3 egg whites
1 cup chilled whipping cream, stiffly beaten

1. Using a spatula, spread the peanut butter on the bottom and sides of the pastry shell. Set aside.
2. Soften gelatin in the cold water and set aside.
3. Combine pumpkin, sugar, milk, egg yolks, spices, and salt in the top of a double boiler. Cook over medium heat 5 minutes. Stir in softened gelatin and cook 5 minutes more. Cool.
4. Beat the egg whites until soft peaks are formed. Gently fold egg whites into thoroughly cooled pumpkin filling. Pour mixture into pie shell. Chill until set.
5. To serve, cut in wedges and top each piece with a swirl of whipped cream.

8 to 10 servings

Lemon Cream Chiffon Tarts

1¼ cups sugar
2 tablespoons cornstarch
1 envelope unflavored gelatin
¼ teaspoon salt
1 cup water
3 egg yolks
½ cup fresh lemon juice
2 tablespoons butter or margarine
1 cup whipping cream
1 teaspoon freshly grated lemon peel
3 egg whites
6 baked 4-inch tart shells
Satin Chocolate Sauce

1. Thoroughly combine 1 cup sugar, cornstarch, gelatin, and salt in a saucepan. Blend in water until smooth.
2. Beat egg yolks until light. Blend with lemon juice into mixture in saucepan. Add butter. Bring to boiling, stirring constantly; continue cooking 2 to 3 minutes. Remove from heat.
3. Stir filling vigorously while gradually adding ⅓ cup whipping cream and grated lemon peel. Immediately pour filling into a cool bowl. Chill until thickened, but not set. (Mixture should mound slightly when dropped from a spoon.)
4. Beat egg whites until soft peaks are formed. Add remaining ¼ cup sugar, beating until egg whites are stiff, but not dry. Whip remaining ⅔ cup whipping cream until stiff.
5. Gently fold egg whites and whipped cream into chilled mixture; mixing thoroughly. Spoon into tart shells. Chill until firm.
6. Drizzle the chocolate sauce over tarts before serving. Serve with additional sauce, if desired.

Six 4-inch tarts

Note: Filling may be poured into a baked 9-inch pastry shell, if desired.

Satin Chocolate Sauce: Heat ½ cup semisweet chocolate pieces with ½ cup light corn syrup over low heat, stirring until chocolate is melted and sauce is smooth. Quickly blend in ¼ cup evaporated milk. Heat 1 minute and cool.

Fresh Lemon Meringue Pie, 63;
Lemon Cream Chiffon Tarts, 65

Cherry-Berry-Peach Pie

3 cups sliced peeled peaches
1 cup fresh blueberries
1 cup halved and pitted fresh sweet
    cherries
1 tablespoon fresh lemon juice
¼ cup firmly packed light brown
    sugar
½ cup granulated sugar
3 tablespoons flour
⅛ teaspoon salt
¼ teaspoon cinnamon
    Cheese Pastry for 2-Crust Pie
      (page 63)
    Milk
    Granulated sugar

1. Combine the peaches, blueberries, and cherries in a large bowl. Sprinkle with lemon juice.
2. Stir together the brown sugar, ½ cup granulated sugar, flour, salt, and cinnamon. Gently stir into fruit, coating fruit evenly.
3. Roll out half the pastry and place in a 9-inch pie pan. Trim pastry so it extends 1 inch beyond rim of pan. Turn fruit into pan.
4. Roll out remaining pastry to form a rectangle about ⅛ inch thick and at least 10 inches long. Cut in ¾-inch strips, using a sharp knife or pastry wheel. Arrange strips in lattice fashion.
5. Trim strips even with edge of bottom crust. Moisten edge with water and fold edge of bottom crust over ends of strips. Flute as desired. Brush top with milk and sprinkle with ¼ to ½ teaspoon sugar.
6. Bake at 450°F 10 minutes. Turn oven control to 350°F and bake 45 to 50 minutes, or until pastry is brown and fruit is tender. Serve warm or cool.

One 9-inch pie

Glazed Strawberry Tart

⅓ cup sugar
3 tablespoons cornstarch
¼ teaspoon salt
⅓ cup instant nonfat dry milk
1½ cups milk
2 eggs, beaten
½ teaspoon grated lemon peel
½ teaspoon vanilla extract
¼ cup white grape juice
1 baked 9-inch pie or tart shell
2 pints ripe strawberries, rinsed,
    hulled, and thoroughly dried
⅓ cup currant jelly
1 tablespoon sugar

1. Combine ⅓ cup sugar with the cornstarch and salt in a heavy saucepan; mix well.
2. Blend the nonfat dry milk with the milk and stir into the cornstarch mixture until smooth. Bring mixture to boiling, stirring constantly; boil 2 to 3 minutes, continuing to stir.
3. Vigorously stir about 3 tablespoons of the hot mixture into the eggs; return to mixture in saucepan. Cook and stir over low heat about 3 minutes, or until very thick.
4. Remove from heat and stir in lemon peel and vanilla extract. Cool slightly, then beat in the white grape juice with a hand rotary or electric beater until blended.
5. Spread the cooled filling in the completely cooled baked pie shell and refrigerate until thoroughly chilled. Top with the strawberries; set aside.
6. Heat jelly until melted and continue to cook about 5 minutes. Spoon over strawberries on the tart filling. Just before serving, sprinkle remaining 1 tablespoon sugar over the tart.

One 9-inch tart

Cakes and Cake Desserts

Angel Food Cake

1 cup sifted cake flour
¾ cup sugar
1½ cups (about 12) egg whites
1 teaspoon cream of tartar
½ teaspoon salt
1 teaspoon vanilla extract
½ teaspoon almond extract
¾ cup sugar

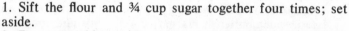

1. Sift the flour and ¾ cup sugar together four times; set aside.
2. Beat egg whites with cream of tartar, salt, and extracts until stiff, not dry, peaks are formed. Lightly fold in remaining sugar, 2 tablespoons at a time.
3. Gently folding until blended after each addition, sift about 4 tablespoons of the flour mixture at a time over meringue. Carefully slide batter into an ungreased 10-inch tube pan, turning pan as batter is poured. Cut through batter with knife or spatula to break large air bubbles.
4. Bake at 350°F about 45 minutes, or until cake tests done.
5. Immediately invert pan and cool cake completely. Cut around cake with a pointed knife, loosen gently with a spatula, and remove cake from pan.

One 10-inch tube cake

Cherry-Nut Angel Food Cake: Follow recipe for Angel Food Cake. Fold in **½ cup finely chopped nuts** and **¼ cup finely chopped, well-drained maraschino cherries** with last addition of flour mixture.

Rainbow Angel Food Cake: Follow recipe for Angel Food Cake. Divide batter equally among 3 bowls. Fold **2 drops red food coloring** into one portion, **2 drops yellow food coloring** and **¼ teaspoon lemon extract** into another, and **2 drops green food coloring and ¼ teaspoon peppermint extract** into the third portion. Form 3 layers in pan.

Toasty-Coconut Angel Food Cake: Follow recipe for Angel Food Cake. Fold in **1 cup toasted flaked coconut** with last addition of flour mixture.

Boston Cream Pie

1 cup sifted cake flour
1 teaspoon baking powder
¼ teaspoon salt
1 cup sugar
3 eggs, well beaten
2 or 3 teaspoons lemon juice
6 tablespoons hot milk (do not boil)
Creamy Vanilla Filling
¼ cup confectioners' sugar

1. Sift the flour, baking powder, and salt together.
2. Add sugar gradually to the beaten eggs, beating until very thick and piled softly. Mix in lemon juice.
3. Sprinkle dry ingredients over egg mixture about one fourth at a time; gently fold in until just blended after each addition.
4. Add hot milk all at one time and quickly mix just until smooth. Turn batter into 2 greased (bottom only) 9-inch layer cake pans.
5. Bake at 375°F 15 to 25 minutes, or until cake tests done.
6. Cool 8 to 10 minutes in pan on wire rack. Remove cake from pan and cool completely on rack.
7. Place one cake layer on serving plate and spread with chilled filling. Cover with second cake layer. Sift confectioners' sugar over top of cake. For a lacy design, sift confectioners' sugar over a lace paper doily on top of cake; carefully remove doily.

One 9-inch layer cake

Creamy Vanilla Filling

⅓ cup sugar
2½ tablespoons flour
¼ teaspoon salt
1½ cups cream or half-and-half
3 egg yolks, slightly beaten
1 tablespoon butter or margarine
2 teaspoons vanilla extract
¼ teaspoon almond extract

1. Mix the sugar, flour, and salt in a heavy saucepan. Stir constantly while gradually adding cream. Bring to boiling; stir and cook 3 minutes.
2. Vigorously stir about 3 tablespoons of the hot mixture into the egg yolks; immediately blend into mixture in saucepan. Stir and cook about 1 minute.
3. Remove from heat and blend in remaining ingredients. Press a circle of waxed paper onto top (this prevents a film from forming). Cool slightly, then chill.

About 1½ cups filling

Apple Lane Cake

1 cup butter or margarine, softened
1 teaspoon vanilla extract
1½ cups sugar
2½ cups all-purpose flour
2 teaspoons baking powder
¼ teaspoon salt
⅔ cup milk
8 egg whites (reserve yolks for filling)
½ cup shredded pared Red or Golden Delicious apples
Apple Filling
White Frosting

1. Cream butter, vanilla extract, and sugar in a large bowl. Mix flour, baking powder, and salt. Blend into creamed mixture alternately with milk.
2. Beat egg whites until stiff, but not dry. Stir a little beaten egg white into batter. Stir in shredded apple. Fold batter into remaining egg whites. Turn into 3 greased and floured 9-inch round layer cake pans.
3. Bake at 350°F 20 to 25 minutes, or until cake tester inserted in center comes out clean. Cool 10 minutes; turn out of pans and cool completely on wire racks.
4. Spread Apple Filling between layers and on top of cake. Frost sides of cake with White Frosting. Refrigerate until ready to serve.

10 to 12 servings

Apple Filling

- **8 egg yolks**
- **1 cup sugar**
- **¼ teaspoon salt**
- **½ cup bourbon**
- **½ cup butter or margarine, melted and cooled**
- **1 teaspoon vanilla extract**
- **1 cup chopped pecans**
- **2 cups chopped Red or Golden Delicious apples**

1. Beat egg yolks, sugar, and salt in a large bowl until light and thick. Gradually beat in bourbon, then butter.
2. Pour mixture into a heavy 2-quart saucepan. Cook, stirring constantly, until thickened (about 10 minutes). Remove from heat; stir in vanilla extract and pecans. Chill.
3. When ready to use, stir in apples.

White Frosting

- **½ cup sugar**
- **¼ cup light corn syrup**
- **2 tablespoons water**
- **2 egg whites**
- **1 teaspoon vanilla extract**

1. Mix sugar, corn syrup, and water in a small saucepan. Cover and bring to boiling over medium heat. Uncover and heat to 242°F; do not stir.
2. While syrup is heating, beat egg whites until stiff peaks form. Gradually beat hot syrup into egg whites, beating until stiff enough to spread. Beat in vanilla extract.

Pound Cake

- **2 cups sifted all-purpose flour**
- **¾ teaspoon baking powder**
- **¼ teaspoon salt**
- **¼ teaspoon mace**
- **1 cup butter**
- **2 teaspoons grated lemon peel**
- **1½ teaspoons vanilla extract**
- **½ teaspoon almond extract**
- **1 cup plus 2 tablespoons sugar**
- **4 eggs, well beaten**

1. Mix together the flour, baking powder, salt, and mace; set aside.
2. Cream butter with lemon peel and extracts until butter is softened. Add sugar gradually, creaming until fluffy after each addition. Add eggs in thirds, beating thoroughly after each addition.
3. Beating only until smooth after each addition, add dry ingredients in fourths to creamed mixture. Turn batter into a greased (bottom only) and waxed-paper-lined (bottom only) 9×5×3-inch loaf pan. With spatula, draw batter from center toward edges of pan.
4. Bake at 325°F 1 hour and 10 minutes, or until wooden pick inserted in center comes out clean. Allow cake to partially cool in pan on wire rack, turn cake out of pan, remove paper, and cool completely.

One 9×5-inch loaf cake

Cherry-Nut Pound Cake: Follow recipe for Pound Cake. Fold in **½ cup finely chopped candied cherries, ¼ cup finely chopped candied citron,** and **¼ cup chopped walnuts** with the last addition of dry ingredients. If desired, fruit may first be marinated in just enough brandy or rum to cover.

Caraway Pound Cake: Follow recipe for Pound Cake. Fold in **1 teaspoon caraway seed** with the last addition of dry ingredients.

Soft Gingerbread

3 cups sifted all-purpose flour
1 teaspoon baking soda
¼ teaspoon salt
2 teaspoons ground cinnamon
2 teaspoons ground ginger
1 teaspoon ground cloves
¼ teaspoon ground nutmeg
½ cup butter
1 cup sugar
2 eggs, well beaten
1 cup light molasses
¼ cup boiling water
1 cup sour milk (see Note)

1. Sift the flour, baking soda, salt, and spices together and blend thoroughly; set aside.
2. Cream butter; gradually add sugar, creaming until fluffy. Add eggs in thirds, beating well after each addition. Add a mixture of molasses and boiling water gradually, mixing well.
3. Beating only until smooth after each addition, alternately add dry ingredients in fourths and sour milk in thirds to creamed mixture. Turn batter into a well-greased (bottom only) 13×9×2-inch baking pan.
4. Bake at 350°F about 35 minutes, or until gingerbread tests done.
5. Cool in pan on wire rack. Serve topped with Banana Fluff (page 91), if desired.

One 13×9-inch cake

Note: To sour milk, pour 1 tablespoon vinegar or lemon juice into a 1-cup measure and add enough fresh milk to make 1 cup; stir.

Bittersweet Chocolate Spice Cake

2¼ cups sifted all-purpose flour
2 teaspoons baking powder
½ teaspoon salt
1 teaspoon ground cinnamon
½ teaspoon ground allspice
½ teaspoon ground nutmeg
¼ teaspoon ground coriander
¾ cup butter or margarine
2 teaspoons vanilla extract
½ teaspoon almond extract
2 cups sugar
4 eggs, well beaten
1 cup milk
5 ounces (5 squares) unsweetened chocolate, grated
Caramel Fudge Frosting

1. Sift the flour, baking powder, salt, and spices together and blend thoroughly; set aside.
2. Cream butter with extracts. Gradually add sugar, creaming thoroughly. Add eggs in fourths, beating thoroughly after each addition.
3. Beating only until blended after each addition, alternately add dry ingredients in fourths and milk in thirds to creamed mixture. Fold in chocolate until blended. Turn batter into 2 greased 9-inch round layer cake pans and spread evenly to edges.
4. Bake at 375°F 30 minutes, or until cake tests done.
5. Cool about 10 minutes. Gently run a spatula around sides of pan. Cover cake with a wire rack and invert. Remove pan, turn cake right side up, and cool completely. Fill and frost with Caramel Fudge Frosting.

One 9-inch 2-layer cake

Caramel Fudge Frosting

3 cups lightly packed light brown
    sugar
1 cup milk
½ cup butter or margarine
    Few grains salt
½ ounce (½ square) unsweetened
    chocolate, cut in pieces
1 teaspoon vanilla extract

1. Combine all ingredients except vanilla extract in a heavy 3-quart saucepan. Stir over low heat until sugar is completely dissolved.
2. Increase heat and bring mixture to boiling. Wash down crystals from sides of pan with a pastry brush dipped in water. Set candy thermometer in place. Cook, stirring occasionally, until thermometer registers 234°F, washing down crystals from sides of pan and dipping brush in fresh water each time.
3. Remove from heat and set aside to cool to 110°F, or until just cool enough to hold pan on palm of hand. Do not disturb frosting during cooling.
4. When cool, stir in the extract and beat until creamy and of spreading consistency.

Venetian Crème Torte

2 cups sifted cake flour
½ cup cocoa, sifted
½ teaspoon baking soda
⅛ teaspoon salt
½ cup butter
2 teaspoons vanilla extract
1⅔ cups sugar
3 eggs
1 cup buttermilk
    Venetian Crème Icing

1. Sift the flour, cocoa, baking soda, and salt together and blend thoroughly; set aside.
2. Cream butter and vanilla extract. Add sugar gradually, beating constantly until thoroughly creamed. Add the eggs, one at a time, beating until light and fluffy after each addition.
3. Beating only until blended after each addition, alternately add dry ingredients in thirds and buttermilk in halves to creamed mixture. Divide batter equally among 6 greased 9-inch layer cake pans and spread evenly to edges.
4. Bake at 350°F about 10 minutes, or until torte layers test done.
5. Cool 10 minutes, remove from pans, and cool completely. Spread icing between layers and on top of torte. Refrigerate until ready to serve.

One 9-inch torte

Venetian Crème Icing

½ cup sugar
½ cup all-purpose flour
½ teaspoon salt
1¾ cups milk
1 cup half-and-half or whipping
    cream
1 cup butter
1 teaspoon vanilla extract
1½ cups confectioners' sugar

1. Thoroughly mix sugar, flour, and salt together in a heavy saucepan. Gradually add milk, stirring until smooth. Blend in half-and-half. Stirring constantly, cook over medium heat until very thick; boil 1 minute. Remove from heat.
2. Cover saucepan and place in ice and water; chill until mixture is set.
3. Cream butter with extract. Add half of confectioners' sugar and beat until fluffy.
4. Beat chilled mixture until smooth. Beating thoroughly after each addition, alternately add chilled mixture and remaining confectioners' sugar to butter mixture.

About 4 cups icing

Pineapple Upside-down Cake

Topping:
- ¼ **cup butter or margarine**
- ⅔ **cup lightly packed brown sugar**
- 5 **canned pineapple slices (reserve ½ cup syrup)**
- 5 **maraschino cherries**

Cake batter:
- 1½ **cups sifted cake flour**
- 2 **teaspoons baking powder**
- ½ **teaspoon salt**
- ½ **cup butter or margarine**
- 1 **teaspoon vanilla extract**
- ½ **cup sugar**
- 1 **egg**

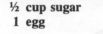

1. For topping, heat butter in an 8×8×2-inch baking pan (or in a 10-inch skillet with a heat-resistant handle); blend in brown sugar and spread evenly. Arrange pineapple slices on top of the brown sugar mixture with a cherry in the center of each. Set aside.

2. For cake batter, sift flour, baking powder, and salt together; set aside.

3. Cream butter with vanilla extract. Add sugar gradually, creaming until fluffy. Add egg and beat thoroughly.

4. Beating only until smooth after each addition, alternately add the dry ingredients in thirds and reserved pineapple syrup in halves to the creamed mixture. Turn batter over pineapple slices and spread evenly to edges of pan.

5. Bake at 350°F about 45 minutes (about 35 minutes for skillet), or until cake tests done.

6. Remove from oven; let stand 1 to 2 minutes in pan on wire rack. Using a spatula, loosen cake from sides of pan and invert onto a serving plate. Allow pan to remain over cake 1 to 2 minutes so syrup will drain onto cake. Remove from pan. Serve warm or cool.

1 upside-down cake

Cranberry Upside-down Cake: Follow recipe for Pineapple Upside-down Cake. In topping, substitute ⅔ **cup granulated sugar** for brown sugar. Blend **1 tablespoon grated orange peel** and ½ **teaspoon vanilla extract** with sugar and butter in pan. Spread mixture evenly in pan. Omit pineapple and cherries; spoon a mixture of **2 cups cranberries,** washed and coarsely chopped, and ⅓ **cup sugar** over mixture in pan. Proceed as directed for cake, substituting ½ **cup milk** for pineapple syrup.

Apricot Upside-down Cake: Follow recipe for Pineapple Upside-down Cake. Substitute the following topping: Simmer ½ **pound dried apricots** in **2 cups water** until fruit is plump and tender. Cool and drain well. Thoroughly blend **3 tablespoons melted butter or margarine,** ½ **cup lightly packed brown sugar,** and ⅓ **cup drained crushed pineapple.** Arrange apricots in lightly greased (bottom only) pan. Spoon pineapple mixture over apricots. Proceed as directed for cake, substituting ½ **cup milk** for pineapple syrup.

Peachy Nut Upside-down Cake: Follow recipe for Apricot Upside-down Cake. Substitute ½ **pound dried peaches** for apricots. Put a **pecan half** in cavity of each peach and arrange nut side down in prepared pan.

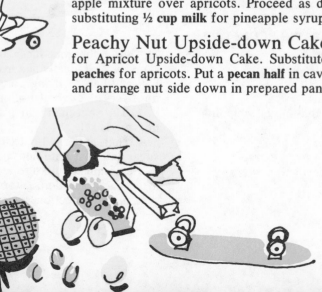

Strawberry Shortcake

1 quart fresh strawberries
½ cup sugar
1¾ cups all-purpose flour
2 tablespoons sugar
1 tablespoon baking powder
½ teaspoon salt
½ cup lard, chilled
¾ cup milk
Melted butter
Milk
Softened butter or margarine
Sweetened whipped cream or
  whipped dessert topping

1. Sort, rinse, and drain the strawberries. Set aside about 14 strawberries; chill. Hull remaining berries. Slice larger berries and leave smaller ones whole. Sprinkle hulled berries with ½ cup sugar. Mix lightly and let stand about 1 hour.
2. Blend flour, 2 tablespoons sugar, baking powder, and salt in a bowl. Cut in the lard with a pastry blender or two knives until particles are about the size of coarse cornmeal. Make a well in the center and add milk all at one time. Stir with a fork 20 to 30 strokes.
3. Turn dough out onto a lightly floured surface and shape it into a ball. Knead lightly with fingertips about 15 times.
4. Divide dough into halves. Roll each half about ¼ inch thick to fit an 8-inch round layer cake pan. Place one round of dough in pan and brush with melted butter. Cover with the other round and brush top with milk.
5. Bake at 425°F 15 to 18 minutes, or until top is delicately browned. Split shortcake while hot into two layers and spread with butter.
6. Place bottom layer, buttered side up, on serving plate. Cover with half of the sweetened berries. Spoon sweetened whipped cream over berries. Cover with top layer, buttered side down, and arrange remaining berries over it. Spoon additional whipped cream on top.
7. Garnish with reserved whole berries. Cut in wedges to serve.

6 servings

Peach Shortcake: Follow recipe for Strawberry Shortcake. Substitute **fresh peach slices** for strawberries.

Sunshine Shortcake: Follow recipe for Strawberry Shortcake. Substitute **orange sections** and **sliced bananas** for strawberries. Sweeten with **confectioners' sugar.**

Pecan Fruitcake

1 pound (about 2½ cups) candied
  red cherries, cut in pieces
1 pound (about 3 cups) golden
  raisins
1 pound (about 4 cups) pecans,
  coarsely chopped
4 cups sifted all-purpose flour
2 teaspoons baking powder
2 cups butter or margarine
4 teaspoons lemon juice
2¼ cups sugar
6 large eggs

1. Combine cherries, raisins, pecans, and 1 cup of the flour. Blend the remaining flour with the baking powder; set aside.
2. Cream butter with lemon juice. Add sugar gradually, creaming until fluffy after each addition. Add eggs, one at a time, beating thoroughly after each addition.
3. Beating only until smooth after each addition, add flour mixture in fourths to creamed mixture. Blend in the fruit mixture. Turn batter into a well-greased 10-inch tube pan and spread evenly.
4. Place a shallow pan containing water on bottom rack of oven during baking time.
5. Bake at 275°F about 4½ hours, or until cake tests done. Set pan on wire rack. Remove from pan before entirely cooled. Cool completely.

About 7 pounds fruitcake

Jelly Roll

⅓ cup (about 4) egg yolks
½ cup sugar
¼ cup water
1½ teaspoons vanilla extract
1 cup sifted cake flour
½ cup (about 4) egg whites
½ teaspoon cream of tartar
¼ teaspoon salt
½ cup sugar
Confectioners' sugar (about 1 cup)
Jelly or jam

1. Grease bottom of a 15×10×1-inch jelly-roll pan; line with waxed paper cut to fit bottom of pan; grease paper. Set aside.
2. Beat egg yolks, ½ cup sugar, water, and vanilla extract together until very thick. Fold in flour until just blended.
3. Beat egg whites with cream of tartar and salt until frothy. Add ½ cup sugar gradually, continuing to beat until stiff peaks are formed.
4. Fold egg-yolk mixture into meringue until blended. Turn batter into the prepared pan and spread evenly.
5. Bake at 350°F 20 to 25 minutes, or until cake tests done.
6. Loosen edges of cake and immediately turn onto a towel with confectioners' sugar sifted over it. Peel off the paper and trim any crisp edges of cake.
7. To roll, begin at a short side of cake. Using towel as a guide, tightly grasp nearest edge of towel and quickly pull it over beyond opposite edge. Cake will roll itself as you pull. Wrap roll in towel and set on wire rack to cool about 30 minutes.
8. When ready to fill, carefully unroll cooled cake, spread with jelly, and reroll.

8 to 10 servings

Chocolate Cake Roll: Follow recipe for Jelly Roll. Decrease cake flour to ¾ cup and sift with **5 tablespoons cocoa.** Bake at 325°F about 30 minutes, or until cake tests done. Fill with **Cocoa Whipped Cream** (page 93), and reroll. Sift **confectioners' sugar or cocoa** over top.

Custard-Filled Cake Roll: Follow recipe for Jelly Roll. Omit jelly or jam. Prepare Vanilla Custard Filling. Stir chopped **black walnuts** or chopped **salted pecans, pistachio nuts, almonds,** or **other nuts** into filling. (If using salted nuts, omit salt in filling.) Fill cake roll and sift **confectioners' sugar or cocoa** over top. If desired, halved, hulled, thoroughly rinsed, and drained **fresh strawberries** may be substituted for nuts in the filling. Garnish with whole strawberries with stems.

Vanilla Custard Filling

½ cup sugar
2 tablespoons cornstarch
¼ teaspoon salt
½ cup cold milk
1 cup milk, scalded
4 egg yolks, beaten
2 teaspoons vanilla extract

1. Mix sugar, cornstarch, and salt together in the top of a double boiler. Blend in cold milk, stirring until mixture is smooth.
2. Add scalded milk gradually, stirring constantly. Bring mixture rapidly to boiling over direct heat and cook 3 minutes, stirring constantly. Remove from heat.
3. Stir about 3 tablespoons of the hot mixture into egg yolks; immediately blend into mixture in double boiler. Set over boiling water and cook about 5 minutes, stirring constantly.
4. Remove from heat; blend in vanilla extract. Cool slightly; refrigerate until ready to use.

About 1½ cups filling

Chocolate Dessert Superb à la Belgique

8 ounces sweet chocolate
7 tablespoons double-strength coffee
½ cup (about 7) egg yolks
¾ cup sugar
1 teaspoon vanilla extract
1 cup (about 7) egg whites
¼ teaspoon salt
¼ cup sugar
2 tablespoons Dutch process cocoa
  Mocha Butter Cream Filling
1 cup chilled whipping cream
3 tablespoons confectioners' sugar
1 teaspoon vanilla extract

1. Grease bottom of a 15×10×1-inch jelly-roll pan; line bottom with waxed paper, allowing paper to extend about 1 inch beyond ends of pan. Grease waxed paper and set pan aside.
2. Put chocolate and coffee in the top of a double boiler. Set over simmering water until chocolate is melted. Set aside to cool.
3. Combine egg yolks, ¾ cup sugar, and 1 teaspoon vanilla extract in a large bowl; beat until very thick.
4. Using a clean beater, beat egg whites and salt until frothy. Add ¼ cup sugar gradually, beating well after each addition. Beat until stiff peaks are formed.
5. Blend cooled chocolate into egg yolk mixture. Gently stir in egg whites. Turn into prepared pan and spread evenly.
6. Bake at 350°F 15 minutes. Turn off oven. Remove pan after 5 minutes. Set on wire rack until cool.
7. Sift cocoa over a clean towel. Turn dessert onto towel. Carefully remove paper. If desired, let stand about 30 minutes to absorb cocoa flavor. Cover with waxed paper until ready to serve.
8. Prepare Mocha Butter Cream Filling; spread generously over dessert. Cut into 16 equal portions and transfer 8 portions to dessert plates. Top with remaining portions, cocoa side up.
9. Beat the whipping cream until soft peaks are formed. Beat in the confectioners' sugar and 1 teaspoon vanilla extract with final few strokes until blended. Spoon a generous amount over each serving.

8 servings

Note: If desired, the mocha filling may be omitted and additional sweetened whipped cream substituted for the filling.

Mocha Butter Cream Filling

1 cup unsalted butter
2 tablespoons rum
1 to 2 teaspoons almond extract
1 teaspoon vanilla extract
2 cups confectioners' sugar, sifted
3 egg yolks
2 teaspoons instant coffee
1½ teaspoons Dutch process cocoa
2 teaspoons boiling water

1. Beat butter, rum, and extracts in a bowl until blended. Gradually add about 1½ cups of the confectioners' sugar, continuing to beat until fluffy. Beat in egg yolks, one at a time.
2. Blend instant coffee and cocoa in a small cup; add the boiling water and stir until thoroughly mixed; cool. Beat into the butter mixture with the remaining ½ cup confectioners' sugar. Chill until ready to use. Allow to come to room temperature; beat, if necessary, to spreading consistency.

Luscious Lemon Cheese Cake

2⅔ cups zwieback crumbs (about 24 slices)
½ cup confectioners' sugar
1½ teaspoons grated lemon peel
½ cup butter or margarine, softened
2½ pounds cream cheese, softened
1¾ cups sugar
3 tablespoons flour
1½ teaspoons grated lemon peel
½ teaspoon vanilla extract
4 eggs, slightly beaten
2 egg yolks
¼ cup whipping cream

1. Butter bottom and sides of a 9-inch springform pan.
2. Mix crumbs, confectioners' sugar, and lemon peel in a bowl. Using a fork, mix in the butter. Reserve ¾ cup of the mixture for topping. Turn remainder into prepared pan; press crumbs firmly into an even layer on bottom and sides of pan. Set aside.
3. Combine cream cheese, sugar, flour, lemon peel, and vanilla extract in a bowl. Beat until smooth and fluffy. Add the eggs and egg yolks in thirds, beating thoroughly after each addition. Blend in cream.
4. Turn mixture into prepared crust, spreading evenly. Sprinkle reserved crumb mixture over top.
5. Bake at 250°F 2 hours. Turn off heat. Let cake stand in oven about 1 hour.
6. Remove to a wire rack to cool completely. Refrigerate several hours or overnight.
7. To serve, remove springform rim. Cut cake into wedges.

One 9-inch cheese cake

Mandarin-Glazed Cheese Cake

1⅓ cups graham cracker crumbs
5 tablespoons sugar
5 tablespoons butter or margarine, softened
1 package (3 ounces) lemon-flavored gelatin
1 cup very hot water
2 packages (8 ounces each) cream cheese, softened
1 teaspoon vanilla extract
½ cup sugar
1 cup chilled whipping cream
1 can (16 ounces) mandarin oranges, drained (reserve syrup)
2 teaspoons lemon juice
1 teaspoon unflavored gelatin

1. Combine graham cracker crumbs and 5 tablespoons sugar. Using a fork or pastry blender, blend in the butter. Using the back of a spoon, press crumb mixture in the bottom and sides of a buttered 8-inch springform pan.
2. Bake crumb crust at 375°F 8 minutes. Cool.
3. Put lemon-flavored gelatin into a bowl. Add the very hot water and stir until gelatin is completely dissolved; cool. Chill, stirring occasionally, until slightly thicker than thick unbeaten egg white.
4. While gelatin is chilling, combine cream cheese and vanilla extract. Gradually add remaining ½ cup sugar, beating until blended.
5. When gelatin is desired consistency, stir several tablespoons into the cream cheese mixture. Continue adding gelatin mixture slowly, stirring constantly until well blended.
6. Beat the whipping cream in a chilled bowl, using chilled beaters, until it piles softly. Gently fold into the gelatin-cheese mixture. Pour mixture into cooled crust. Chill until set (about 1 hour).
7. While cheesecake is chilling, pour the lemon juice into a small cup. Sprinkle the unflavored gelatin over the juice. Let stand about 5 minutes to soften.
8. Heat the reserved mandarin orange syrup until very hot. Add the softened gelatin and stir until completely dissolved. Cool. Chill gelatin mixture, stirring occasionally, until slightly thicker than thick unbeaten egg white.
9. Arrange mandarin orange segments on top of cheese cake. Spoon glaze evenly over orange segments. Chill until glaze is set.

12 to 16 servings

Small Cakes, Cookies, and Candies

Carrot Cupcakes

1½ cups sifted all-purpose flour
1 teaspoon baking powder
1 teaspoon baking soda
1 teaspoon ground cinnamon
½ teaspoon salt
1 cup sugar
¾ cup vegetable oil
2 eggs
1 cup grated raw carrots
½ cup chopped nuts

1. Blend flour, baking powder, baking soda, cinnamon, and salt. Set aside.
2. Combine sugar and oil in a bowl and beat thoroughly. Add eggs, one at a time, beating thoroughly after each addition. Mix in carrots. Add dry ingredients gradually, beating until blended. Mix in nuts.
3. Spoon into muffin-pan wells, lined with paper baking cups.
4. Bake at 350°F 15 to 20 minutes.

About 16 cupcakes

Chocolate-Coated Party Cakes

4 egg yolks
⅓ cup sugar
1 teaspoon grated lemon peel
4 egg whites
⅓ cup sugar
1 cup sifted cake flour
1 cup sweetened whipped cream
    Chocolate Glaze (page 34)

1. Beat egg yolks, ⅓ cup sugar, and lemon peel until very thick and lemon colored. Set aside.
2. Beat egg whites until frothy; add ⅓ cup sugar gradually, continuing to beat until stiff peaks are formed.
3. Fold egg yolk mixture into beaten whites until blended. Sprinkle about one fourth of the flour at a time over the egg mixture; fold together gently until just blended after each addition.
4. Turn batter into 12 greased (bottoms only) 2½ × 1¼-inch muffin pan wells, filling each about two thirds full.
5. Bake at 325°F 18 minutes, or until delicately browned.
6. Cool slightly; run a spatula gently around sides of cakes; lift out and set on wire racks to cool.
7. Cut a thin slice from bottom of each cake and carefully hollow out the cake. Fill with sweetened whipped cream and replace cake slice. Spoon Chocolate Glaze over tops of cakes and allow glaze to set slightly before serving.

1 dozen small cakes

Pumpkin Miniatures

2¼ cups sifted cake flour
.1 tablespoon baking powder
½ teaspoon baking soda
½ teaspoon salt
1½ teaspoons ground cinnamon
½ teaspoon ground allspice
½ teaspoon ground ginger
½ cup butter or margarine
½ cup sugar
1 cup lightly packed dark brown
   sugar
2 eggs
¾ cup buttermilk
¾ cup canned pumpkin
½ cup finely snipped or chopped
   golden raisins

1. Sift the flour, baking powder, baking soda, salt, and spices together and blend thoroughly; set aside.
2. Cream butter; gradually add sugars, creaming until fluffy. Add eggs, one at a time, beating thoroughly after each addition.
3. Beating only until smooth after each addition, alternately add dry ingredients in fourths and a mixture of the buttermilk, pumpkin, and raisins in thirds to creamed mixture. Spoon batter into 1¾-inch muffin-pan wells lined with paper cups, filling half full.
4. Bake at 375°F about 13 minutes, or until cupcakes test done.
5. Remove from pans and cool on racks. Dust with **confectioners' sugar** before serving.

6½ dozen cupcakes

Ladyfingers

3 egg whites (⅓ cup)
   Few grains salt
⅓ cup sugar
2 egg yolks
¼ teaspoon orange extract
¼ teaspoon vanilla extract
⅓ cup all-purpose flour
   Confectioners' sugar

1. Using an 18×12-inch baking pan, cut both brown and waxed paper to fit the bottom of pan.
2. Cut a ladyfinger pattern from paper or cardboard about 4½ inches long and ¾ inch wide. Trace the pattern on the brown paper in sets of six, forming 4 rows across. (There will be 24 patterns traced on the paper with space between each pattern and between each row.)
3. Place brown paper in the pan and cover with the waxed paper. (The ladyfinger pattern will show through the waxed paper.)
4. Put egg whites and salt into a mixing bowl and beat until frothy; beat in sugar gradually until stiff peaks are formed.
5. Beat egg yolks with extracts until very thick. Add to the meringue, folding gently until well blended. Sift the flour over all, a little at a time, folding gently after each addition.
6. Using a pastry bag, pipe out dumbbell-shaped ladyfingers over the patterns.
7. Bake at 350°F 12 to 15 minutes, or until ladyfingers spring back when lightly touched.
8. Remove from oven and invert over a clean towel sprinkled with some confectioners' sugar. Discard the brown paper and immediately pull the waxed paper from ladyfinger halves. Put ladyfingers together in pairs as soon as they are removed from paper. (After cooling, the halves wll not adhere to each other.) Cool on wire racks and cover with a towel. Store in a covered container.

12 pairs ladyfingers

Banana Fritters with Mocha Sauce

4 firm bananas with all-yellow peel
3 tablespoons confectioners' sugar
2 tablespoons lemon juice
1½ tablespoons rum or kirsch
Mocha Sauce (page 89)
1⅓ cups sifted all-purpose flour
2 tablespoons sugar
1 teaspoon baking powder
½ teaspoon salt
2 egg yolks
1 tablespoon shortening, melted and cooled
⅔ cup milk
1 teaspoon vanilla extract
2 egg whites
¼ cup all-purpose flour
Vegetable shortening, lard, or oil for deep-frying heated to 365°F

1. Peel bananas and cut crosswise into 1½-inch pieces. Gently toss banana pieces with a mixture of confectioners' sugar, lemon juice, and rum. Cover the bowl and allow banana pieces to marinate 45 minutes to 1 hour, turning fruit occasionally.
2. While bananas are marinating, prepare Mocha Sauce and keep warm in the top of a double boiler over simmering water.
3. Mix together the sifted flour, sugar, baking powder, and salt.
4. Drain banana pieces and set aside, reserving liquid. Beat egg yolks until thick and lemon colored. Beat in the melted shortening, reserved liquid from the bananas, milk, and vanilla extract.
5. Make a well in center of dry ingredients. Pour in liquid mixture all at one time and blend just until batter is smooth. Beat egg whites until they form rounded peaks. Gently fold into batter.
6. Coat banana pieces by rolling in ¼ cup flour. Using a large fork or slotted spoon, dip banana pieces into batter and coat evenly. Drain excess batter from pieces before deep-frying.
7. Deep-fry only as many fritters at one time as will float uncrowded in one layer. Turn fritters with a fork as they rise to the surface and several times during cooking, being careful not to pierce fritters. Deep-fry 2 to 3 minutes, or until golden brown. Drain fritters over fat a few seconds before removing to absorbent paper.
8. Serve immediately topped with warm sauce.

5 or 6 servings

Apple Fritters: Follow recipe for Banana Fritters. Substitute **5 medium apples** for bananas. Wash, core, pare, and cut apples into crosswise ¼-inch slices to form rings.

Strawberry Fritters: Follow recipe for Banana Fritters. Substitute for the bananas **1 quart large firm strawberries,** rinsed and hulled. Do not marinate the berries. Add the rum to the batter; omit lemon juice. Increase confectioners' sugar to ½ cup and roll berries in it instead of rolling in flour, before dipping in batter. Increase flour in batter to 1½ cups. Do not serve with Mocha Sauce. Just before serving, sprinkle fritters with about ¼ cup **Vanilla Confectioners' Sugar.**

Vanilla Confectioners' Sugar: Cut a **vanilla bean** lengthwise, then crosswise, into pieces. Poke pieces into **1 to 2 pounds confectioners' sugar** at irregular intervals. Cover tightly and store. (The longer the sugar stands, the richer the flavor.) When necessary, add more sugar. Replace vanilla bean when aroma is gone.

Fresh Fruit Fondue

⅔ cup all-purpose flour
2 tablespoons sugar
1 tablespoon cornstarch
½ teaspoon baking powder
¼ teaspoon salt
½ cup milk
1 egg
  Oil for deep-frying
  Bananas, peeled and cut in 1-inch pieces
  Apples, peaches, or pears, cored, pared, and sliced
  Caramel Sauce, confectioners' sugar, or maple-flavored syrup

1. Combine flour, sugar, cornstarch, baking powder, and salt in a bowl; mix well. Add a mixture of milk and egg. Beat batter until smooth. Pour into a small serving bowl. If desired, batter may be mixed by placing all ingredients in a blender jar and blending until smooth.
2. Heat oil in a fondue pot, if available, or in a saucepan on the range, to 365°F. Spear a piece of fruit, dip in batter, drain off excess, and hold in hot oil until golden brown.
3. Serve warm with Caramel Sauce.

4 to 6 servings

Caramel Sauce: Cream **2 tablespoons soft butter or margarine** with **¾ cup firmly packed brown sugar.** Stir in **¼ teaspoon salt** and **½ cup hot evaporated milk.** Stir until blended.

1¼ cups sauce

Apple Rosettes

¾ cup all-purpose flour
1 tablespoon grated lemon peel
1 teaspoon sugar
1 teaspoon nutmeg
1 teaspoon salt
1 apple, pared and cored
1 cup milk
2 egg yolks
1 tablespoon cooking oil
  Fat for deep frying heated to 375°F
  Confectioners' sugar

1. Stir together the flour, lemon peel, sugar, nutmeg, and salt. Set aside.
2. Purée the apple in a blender or force through a food mill. Add milk, egg yolks, and oil to puréed apple. Beat apple mixture into dry ingredients, using a wire whisk or wooden spoon, until smooth.
3. Prepare rosette iron by dipping in preheated oil. Tap gently to remove excess oil. Lower hot iron into batter, not more than three fourths the depth of the iron (if batter goes over top, cookie will be difficult to remove). Lower coated iron into hot fat and fry until delicately browned (about 30 seconds). Remove from fat and slip cookie from iron.
4. Drain, inverted, on paper towels. Repeat process until all batter is used. Dip cookies while warm in confectioners' sugar.

About 4 dozen rosettes

Chocolate-Bran Brownies

¾ cup sifted all-purpose flour
¼ teaspoon baking soda
¼ teaspoon salt
⅓ cup vegetable shortening
½ cup sugar
2 tablespoons water
1 package (6 ounces) semisweet chocolate pieces
1 teaspoon vanilla extract
2 eggs
½ cup whole bran cereal or whole bran cereal with wheat germ
½ cup coarsely chopped nuts

1. Combine flour, baking soda, and salt. Set aside.
2. Place shortening, sugar, and water in a saucepan. Bring to boiling over moderate heat, stirring constantly. Remove from heat immediately.
3. Add semisweet chocolate pieces and vanilla extract; stir until chocolate pieces are melted. Add eggs and beat well.
4. Add flour mixture, cereal, and nuts; mix well. Spread batter in a greased 8×8×2-inch baking pan.
5. Bake at 325°F about 25 minutes, or until a wooden pick inserted near center comes out clean. Cool thoroughly in pan on wire rack before cutting in squares.

16 squares

Apple Lane Cake, 68

Scotch Shortbread

1 cup butter or margarine
½ cup sugar
3½ cups sifted all-purpose flour

1. Cream butter until softened. Gradually add sugar, creaming until fluffy after each addition. Add the flour gradually, beating until well blended (mixture will be crumbly).
2. Divide mixture evenly between two 9-inch pie pans. With fingers, press dough into pans and with knife handle make indentations around edges about ½ inch apart. Mark each shortbread into wedges and prick with a fork.
3. Bake at 300°F about 30 minutes, or until lightly browned. Remove pans to cooling racks and cool slightly. Cut shortbread into wedges, remove from pans, and cool thoroughly.

16 large cookie wedges

Elegant Date Fingers

¾ pound (about 2 cups) pitted dates, cut in pieces
1 cup hot water
½ cup orange juice
½ cup chopped pecans
¾ cup butter
1 teaspoon grated orange peel
⅛ teaspoon almond extract
⅔ cup firmly packed brown sugar
1½ cups sifted all-purpose flour
¾ teaspoon baking soda
¼ teaspoon salt
1¼ cups uncooked oats
2 tablespoons confectioners' sugar

1. Invert a 9×9-inch pan onto a piece of waxed paper. Using a knife, outline the pan without cutting through the paper and set aside. Turn pan up and grease the bottom.
2. Combine dates, water, and orange juice in a saucepan. Cook over medium heat, stirring occasionally, about 15 minutes, or until mixture is blended and thick. Stir in pecans and set aside.
3. Cream butter with orange peel and almond extract; add brown sugar gradually, beating until fluffy.
4. Sift together flour, baking soda, and salt; add in thirds to creamed mixture, mixing until blended after each addition. Stir in oats.
5. Spread half the mixture in an even layer in the bottom of the pan. Spread date filling over dough to within ¼ inch of sides of the pan; pat remaining dough to fit square on marked-off waxed paper. Invert waxed paper on top of filling and press down gently; carefully peel off waxed paper.
6. Bake at 400°F 20 to 25 minutes, or until golden brown. Cool completely; cut into bars and remove from pan. Sift the confectioners' sugar over bars.

About 3 dozen bars

Note: For a special touch, cut into diamond shapes and decorate with **pink butter frosting rosettes** and **green butter frosting leaves.** For a dessert, cut into large squares and top with **whipped cream.**

Walnut Brittle, 85; Lime-Walnut Divinity, 85;
Walnut Marshmallows, 86; Walnut Toffee, 84

Nutty Raspberry Squares

1 roll (18 ounces) refrigerator
    dough for sugar cookies (at
    room temperature)
1½ cups quick-cooking oats
1 cup chopped walnuts
1 jar (10 ounces) raspberry
    preserves
2 teaspoons grated lemon peel
1 tablespoon lemon juice

1. Crumble cookie dough into pieces. Cut in oats and nuts with a pastry blender or two knives.
2. Pat mixture into an ungreased 9-inch square baking pan, reserving about one quarter of the mixture for topping.
3. Combine preserves, lemon peel, and lemon juice; pour over dough in baking pan. Crumble remaining dough mixture into small pieces and sprinkle over top.
4. Bake at 375°F 25 to 30 minutes. Cool in pan and cut in squares.

About 2 dozen squares

Golden Lemon Squares

2¼ cups sifted all-purpose flour
1 teaspoon baking powder
1 cup butter or margarine, melted
    and cooled
1½ teaspoons vanilla extract
¾ teaspoon lemon extract
1¼ cups sugar
4 eggs
1 cup mashed cooked carrots,
    cooled
Lemon Glaze

1. Blend flour and baking powder.
2. Put butter and extracts into bowl of electric mixer and add sugar gradually, beating thoroughly. Add eggs, one at a time, beating well after each addition.
3. Add carrots and flour mixture; beat 1 minute. Turn into a greased 15×10×1-inch jelly-roll pan.
4. Bake at 350°F about 25 minutes.
5. Cool in pan on wire rack. Spread with glaze; let stand until glaze is set. Cut into squares.

5 to 6 dozen cookies

Lemon Glaze: Beat together **2¼ cups confectioners' sugar, 3 tablespoons lemon juice,** and **1 tablespoon water.**

Frosted Cashew Clusters

2 cups sifted all-purpose flour
½ teaspoon baking powder
¼ teaspoon baking soda
¼ teaspoon salt
½ cup butter
½ teaspoon vanilla extract
1 cup firmly packed brown sugar
1 egg, well beaten
⅓ cup dairy sour cream
1¾ cups salted cashews, coarsely
    chopped
Golden Butter Frosting
Cashew halves

1. Sift the flour, baking powder, baking soda, and salt together.
2. Cream butter with vanilla extract until butter is softened. Add sugar gradually, creaming until fluffy after each addition. Add egg gradually, beating thoroughly.
3. Mixing until blended after each addition, alternately add dry ingredients in fourths and sour cream in thirds to creamed mixture. Mix in the chopped nuts. Drop by teaspoonfuls about 2 inches apart onto a greased cookie sheet; flatten slightly.
4. Bake at 350°F 12 minutes. Remove cookies to wire racks. Frost when cool and top each cookie with a cashew half.

About 9 dozen cookies

Golden Butter Frosting: Heat **½ cup butter** until browned. Remove from heat and stir in **3 tablespoons half-and-half** and **¼ teaspoon lemon extract.** Stir butter mixture into **2 cups sifted confectioners' sugar.** Beat until frosting reaches desired consistency.

Granola Cookies with Raisins

1½ cups sifted all-purpose flour
1 teaspoon baking soda
1¾ cups regular granola
1 cup firmly packed brown sugar
½ cup granulated sugar
1 cup butter or margarine (at room temperature)
1 teaspoon vanilla extract
1 egg
1 cup dark or golden raisins

1. Combine the flour and baking soda in a large bowl of electric mixer. Add granola, sugars, soft butter, vanilla extract, and egg. Mix at low speed until blended, then mix at medium speed 2 minutes, scraping bowl occasionally. Stir in raisins.
2. Drop by teaspoonfuls onto greased cookie sheets.
3. Bake at 375°F about 12 minutes. Cool cookies on wire racks.

About 8 dozen cookies

Golden Harvest Hazelnut Cookies

1 cup butter
1 cup sugar
2 eggs
1 cup all-purpose flour
2½ cups ground hazelnuts (filberts may be used)
1 egg, beaten (for brushing cookies)

1. Cream butter with sugar. Add eggs, one at a time, beating thoroughly after each addition. Mix in flour and nuts. Chill thoroughly, preferably overnight.
2. Shape mixture into bars about 3 inches long, 1 inch wide, and ½ inch thick. Brush with beaten egg. Arrange on greased cookie sheets.
3. Bake at 350°F 10 to 15 minutes. Cool cookies on wire rack.

About 3 dozen cookies

Tropichocolate Wafers

1½ cups sifted all-purpose flour
½ teaspoon baking soda
½ teaspoon salt
½ cup cocoa
½ cup butter or margarine
½ teaspoon vanilla extract
1 cup firmly packed brown sugar
1 egg
¾ cup flaked coconut

1. Blend flour, baking soda, salt, and cocoa. Set aside.
2. Cream butter with vanilla extract. Add brown sugar gradually, creaming until fluffy. Add egg and beat thoroughly.
3. Mixing until well blended after each addition, add dry ingredients in thirds to creamed mixture. Stir in coconut.
4. Chill dough in refrigerator until easy to handle, then shape into 2 rolls about 1½ inches in diameter. Wrap each roll in waxed paper, aluminum foil, or plastic wrap. Chill several hours or overnight.
5. Remove rolls of dough from refrigerator as needed. Cut each roll into ⅛-inch slices. Place slices about 1½ inches apart on lightly greased cookie sheets.
6. Bake at 400°F 5 to 8 minutes. Cool cookies on wire racks.

About 5 dozen cookies

Cranberry Jelly Candy

1 can (16 ounces) jellied cranberry
    sauce
3 packages (3 ounces each) cherry,
    raspberry, or orange-flavored
    gelatin
1 cup sugar
½ of 6-ounce bottle liquid fruit pectin
1 cup chopped nuts
5 to 6 tablespoons sugar

1. Beat cranberry sauce until smooth in a medium saucepan. Bring to boiling over high heat. Stir in gelatin and sugar; simmer 10 minutes, stirring frequently, until sugar is dissolved. Remove from heat.
2. Stir in fruit pectin. Add nuts and stir 10 minutes to prevent nuts from floating. Pour into a buttered 9-inch square pan. Chill until firm (about 2 hours).
3. Run a knife around edge of pan to loosen candy. Invert onto waxed paper, which has been sprinkled with about 2 tablespoons sugar. If candy does not come loose, lift a corner of the candy away from the pan while holding over the waxed paper. Cut candy into ¾-inch squares, using a spatula dipped in warm water. Roll in sugar, and set aside on waxed paper.
4. After candy has dried a little (about 1 hour), roll again in sugar, if desired. Store in a tightly covered container in a cool place.

About 2 pounds candy

Walnut Toffee

2¼ cups walnut pieces
2 cups granulated sugar
½ cup water
½ cup light corn syrup
1 cup butter
1 package (6 ounces) semisweet or
    milk chocolate pieces (may use
    half of each)

1. Coarsely chop 1½ cups walnuts for the toffee. Finely chop the remaining walnuts and set aside for the topping.
2. Combine sugar, water, corn syrup, and butter. Bring to boiling, stirring until sugar is dissolved. Cover and cook 5 minutes. Uncover and boil to 300°F (hard crack stage). Remove from heat.
3. Stir in the coarsely chopped walnuts and quickly spread in a buttered 15×10×1-inch jelly-roll pan. Let stand until cooled.
4. Melt chocolate pieces over warm (not hot) water. Spread over cooled toffee. Sprinkle finely chopped walnuts over chocolate. Let stand until chocolate is set (about 30 minutes). Break into pieces.

About 2½ pounds candy

Mixed Fruit Bars

1 package (11 ounces) mixed dried
    fruits
1 cup butter or margarine, softened
½ cup granulated sugar
2⅔ cups sifted all-purpose flour
1 teaspoon baking powder
½ teaspoon salt
1¾ cups firmly packed brown sugar
4 eggs, slightly beaten
1 teaspoon vanilla extract
1 cup chopped pecans or walnuts
Confectioners' sugar

1. Cook fruit according to package directions. Drain, cool, and chop.
2. Mix butter, granulated sugar, and 2 cups flour until mixture is crumbly. Press into a greased 13×9-inch baking pan.
3. Bake at 350°F 20 to 25 minutes.
4. Sift remaining ⅔ cup flour with baking powder and salt. Gradually beat brown sugar into eggs. Add flour mixture; mix well. Add vanilla extract, nuts, and fruit. Spread over baked base.
5. Bake at 350°F 40 to 45 minutes, or until browned. Cool, cut into bars, and dust with confectioners' sugar.

4 dozen bars

Walnut Brittle

2 cups sugar
1 cup light or dark corn syrup
½ cup water
1 teaspoon salt
2 tablespoons butter
3 cups coarsely chopped walnuts
2 teaspoons baking soda

1. Combine sugar, corn syrup, water, salt, and butter in a saucepan. Cook over moderate heat, stirring until sugar is dissolved. Cover and simmer 5 minutes to wash down sugar crystals from side of pan.
2. Uncover and boil to 300°F (hard crack stage).
3. While syrup is cooking, spread walnuts in a shallow pan and toast lightly in a 300°F oven. When candy reaches 300°F, quickly stir in the warm walnuts and baking soda. Turn at once into an oiled 15×10×1-inch jelly-roll pan (or two oiled cookie sheets if thinner brittle is desired) and spread thin.
4. Let stand until cold, then break into pieces.

About 2 pounds candy

Lime-Walnut Divinity

3 cups granulated sugar
1 cup water
¼ cup light corn syrup
¼ teaspoon salt
2 egg whites
1 package (3 ounces) lime-flavored gelatin
1 tablespoon lime juice
1 cup coarsely chopped walnuts

1. Combine the sugar, water, corn syrup, and salt in a large saucepan. Stir over moderate heat until sugar dissolves.
2. Cover saucepan and boil slowly 3 or 4 minutes, so steam will dissolve any sugar crystals on sides of pan. Uncover and boil over moderate heat until mixture reaches 248°F (firm ball stage).
3. When syrup reaches 248°F continue cooking, but beat egg whites until stiff. Gradually add gelatin, beating to form stiff peaks. Beat in lime juice. Set aside until syrup reaches 260°F (hard ball stage).
4. Begin beating the egg-white mixture and slowly pour in the hot syrup. Do not scrape sides of saucepan. Continue beating until mixture loses its gloss. Quickly stir in walnuts and drop by large teaspoonfuls onto waxed paper, or turn into an oiled 9-inch square pan.
5. Let candy stand until firm, then cut in squares. Store in a tightly covered container.

About 1 pound candy

Note: For raspberry or strawberry divinity, use **raspberry-** or **strawberry-flavored gelatin,** and substitute **lemon juice** for lime juice.

Favorite Fudge

2 packages (6 ounces each) semisweet chocolate pieces
2 bars (8 ounces each) milk chocolate, broken in pieces
16 large marshmallows, quartered, or 160 miniature marshmallows (about 4 ounces)
1 can (13 ounces) evaporated milk
4½ cups sugar
¼ cup butter
1 cup chopped pecans
1 tablespoon vanilla extract

1. Combine chocolate and marshmallows in a bowl. Set aside.
2. Put evaporated milk, sugar, and butter into a Dutch oven or large saucepot. Set over low heat and stir until sugar is dissolved. Increase heat and bring to a rolling boil.
3. Cook over medium heat exactly 5 minutes, stirring constantly. Remove from heat and stir in reserved ingredients until completely blended. Stir in pecans and vanilla extract. Immediately turn into a buttered 13×9-inch pan.
4. When fudge is cooled completely, cut into squares.

About 5 pounds candy

Pastel Candied Fruit Peel

3 large grapefruit or 6 oranges (free from blemishes)
Water
2 packages (3 ounces each) or 1 package (6 ounces) fruit-flavored gelatin (any flavor)
2 cups water
1 cup sugar
1 large stick cinnamon
½ teaspoon whole cloves
1 cup sugar

1. Cut grapefruit in halves. Squeeze out juice, strain, and use as desired.
2. Cover grapefruit rinds with water in a saucepan. Cover pan and bring to boiling. Boil 15 minutes; drain. Using a spoon, carefully remove any remaining pulp and white membrane.
3. Using scissors or a sharp knife, cut the peel into thin strips, about ¼ inch wide, or cut into fancy shapes using hors d'oeuvres cutters. Place in a saucepan and cover with water. Boil, covered, 15 minutes, or until easily pierced with a fork. Drain.
4. Mix gelatin with 2 cups water and 1 cup sugar in a heavy 10-inch skillet. Add the fruit peel and spices, stirring to coat with the syrup. Bring to boiling. Reduce heat and continue cooking, stirring occasionally, until peels are translucent and syrup is almost absorbed (about 50 minutes). Remove from heat.
5. Lift peels from the skillet with a fork or slotted spoon and place in a single layer on wire racks over trays to drain. Let stand 1 hour or more until surface is dried. Sprinkle with 1 cup sugar (use more if needed) and toss lightly. Arrange pieces in a single layer on waxed-paper-lined trays. Let dry about 12 hours or overnight. Store in a tightly covered container.

About 1½ pounds

Walnut Marshmallows

1½ cups walnuts
2 envelopes unflavored gelatin
1¼ cups water
2 cups granulated sugar
¼ teaspoon salt
1 teaspoon mint extract
3 to 4 drops green food coloring

1. Finely chop walnuts. Pour 1 cup of the nuts into a 9-inch square pan, and pat in an even layer.
2. Soften gelatin in ½ cup of the water. Combine remaining ¾ cup water with the sugar and salt, and cook until syrup reaches 234°F (soft ball stage). Add softened gelatin and let mixture stand until it cools to 130°F.
3. Add mint extract and food coloring. Beat at high speed with an electric mixer until very thick. Turn into the walnut-layered pan. Sprinkle remaining chopped walnuts on top. Let stand several hours or overnight.
4. Cut into squares and roll sides in any walnuts remaining in pan.

About 1½ pounds candy

Vanilla Marshmallows: Omit coloring and mint extract. Stir in **2 teaspoons vanilla extract.**

Peppermint Marshmallows: Substitute ¼ **teaspoon peppermint extract** for mint extract, and **red food coloring** for the green food coloring.

Sauces

Almond-Butterscotch Sauce

1¼ cups firmly packed light brown
    sugar
⅔ cup chilled whipping cream
⅔ cup light corn syrup
¼ cup butter or margarine
⅛ teaspoon salt
½ cup chopped toasted blanched
    almonds

1. Combine all ingredients except almonds in a heavy 2-quart saucepan; stir over low heat until sugar is dissolved and butter is melted. Increase heat to medium and bring to boiling; stir occasionally.
2. Set a candy thermometer in place. Cook without stirring until thermometer registers 226°F.
3. Remove from heat and cool slightly. Stir in the almonds. Serve warm.

About 2½ cups sauce

Note: Sauce may be stored in a tightly covered container in the refrigerator and reheated before using.

Custard Sauce

⅓ cup sugar
1 teaspoon flour
⅛ teaspoon salt
2 eggs
1 egg yolk
1½ cups milk
1½ teaspoons vanilla extract

1. Combine the sugar, flour, and salt in the top of a double boiler. Add eggs and egg yolk; mix thoroughly. Blend in ¼ cup of the milk.
2. Heat remaining milk just until hot. Blend into mixture in double-boiler top. Stirring constantly, cook over simmering water until mixture coats a metal spoon (about 10 minutes).
3. Remove from water; stir in vanilla extract. Cool; chill at least 3 hours.

About 2 cups sauce

Raisin-Caramel Sauce

3 tablespoons butter
1 cup packed light brown sugar
½ cup cream or half-and-half
½ cup golden raisins, plumped
1 teaspoon vanilla extract

1. Heat butter in a small saucepan. Add brown sugar and stir over low heat until smooth. Remove from heat.
2. Add cream very slowly, stirring until blended after each addition. Heat about 1 minute. Stir in raisins and vanilla extract. Serve warm or chilled.

About 2 cups sauce

Foamy Sauce

2 tablespoons butter
¼ teaspoon vanilla extract
1½ cups confectioners' sugar
1 egg yolk
2 tablespoons milk
1 egg white
1 cup chilled whipping cream, whipped

1. Cream the butter with vanilla extract. Add ¼ cup confectioners' sugar and beat until fluffy. Add the egg yolk and beat thoroughly.
2. Beating until smooth after each addition, alternately add 1 cup confectioners' sugar in thirds and the milk in halves to creamed mixture.
3. Beat the egg white until rounded peaks are formed. Gradually add remaining ¼ cup confectioners' sugar, beating in with final few strokes.
4. Fold whipped cream and beaten egg white into creamed mixture. Chill until ready to serve.

About 3 cups sauce

Vanilla Hard Sauce

⅔ cup butter or margarine
2 teaspoons vanilla extract
2 cups confectioners' sugar
  Few grains salt
2 teaspoons cream or half-and-half

1. Cream butter with vanilla extract. Gradually add confectioners' sugar with salt, beating until fluffy after each addition. Beat in cream.
2. Chill until mixture is stiff enough to force through a pastry bag and tube.

About 1⅓ cups sauce

Note: If desired, press hard sauce evenly into an 8-inch square baking pan. Chill until firm and cut into fancy shapes.

Almond Hard Sauce: Follow recipe for Vanilla Hard Sauce. Substitute ½ **teaspoon almond extract** for the vanilla extract and mix in ½ **cup finely chopped almonds.**

Brandy Hard Sauce: Follow recipe for Vanilla Hard Sauce. Substitute ¼ **cup brandy** for the vanilla extract. Increase confectioners' sugar, if necessary, and omit cream.

Vanilla Sauce

1 cup sugar
2 tablespoons cornstarch
¼ teaspoon salt
2 cups boiling water
¼ cup butter or margarine
2 teaspoons vanilla extract

1. Combine the sugar, cornstarch, and salt in a saucepan. Mix well and add boiling water gradually, stirring constantly. Continue to stir, bring to boiling and simmer 5 minutes.
2. Remove from heat and blend in butter and vanilla extract. Serve warm.

About 2 cups sauce

Lemon Sauce: Follow recipe for Vanilla Sauce. Substitute **3 tablespoons lemon juice** and **2 teaspoons grated lemon peel** for extract.

Brandy Sauce: Follow recipe for Lemon Sauce. Decrease lemon juice to 1 tablespoon and stir in **3 tablespoons brandy.**

Chocolate Sauce

2 ounces (2 squares) **unsweetened chocolate**
6 tablespoons water
½ cup sugar
Few grains salt
2 tablespoons butter
½ teaspoon vanilla extract

1. Combine chocolate and water in a saucepan. Stir over low heat until smooth and blended.
2. Add sugar and salt; stir constantly until sugar is dissolved and mixture thickens slightly (about 5 minutes). Remove from heat.
3. Blend in butter and vanilla extract. Cool slightly.

About 1 cup sauce

Bittersweet Chocolate Sauce Deluxe

1 package (12 ounces) semisweet chocolate pieces
2 ounces (2 squares) unsweetened chocolate
1 cup chilled whipping cream
1 teaspoon vanilla extract

1. Heat all ingredients together in the top of a double boiler set over hot (not steaming) water, stir frequently until smooth.
2. Sauce may be stored, covered, in refrigerator. Serve hot for ice cream sundaes or cool for ice cream sodas.

2 cups sauce

Note: For a cake filling or topping, slowly add **½ cup chilled whipping cream** to **1 cup cooled Bittersweet Chocolate Sauce Deluxe,** beating constantly with an electric beater until light and fluffy.

Mocha Sauce

1 cup sugar
2 cups double-strength coffee
2 tablespoons cornstarch
3 tablespoons butter or margarine
1 teaspoon vanilla extract

1. Melt the sugar in a heavy, light-colored skillet over low heat, stirring constantly. Slowly add 1½ cups coffee, stirring constantly and mixing thoroughly.
2. Stir the cornstarch and 3 tablespoons coffee into the coffee-sugar mixture. Stirring constantly, bring sauce to boiling. Cook 3 to 5 minutes, or until mixture thickens, stirring constantly. Remove from heat.
3. Add butter and vanilla extract, stirring until butter is completely melted and sauce is well blended.

About 2 cups sauce

Fudge Sauce

1⅓ cups undiluted evaporated milk
1 cup sugar
¼ cup butter or margarine
2 ounces (2 squares) unsweetened chocolate
⅛ teaspoon salt
1 tablespoon vanilla extract

1. Combine evaporated milk, sugar, butter, chocolate, and salt in a heavy saucepan. Cook and stir over low heat until sugar is dissolved.
2. Cover and heat 20 minutes, without stirring. Then stir until all ingredients are blended and cook over medium heat until thickened, stirring constantly. Remove from heat and stir in vanilla extract.
3. Serve hot or cool.

About 1½ cups sauce

Note: Sauce becomes very thick after storing in refrigerator. Before serving, reheat over simmering water to restore its original consistency.

Peanut Butter Sundae Sauce Superb

½ cup firmly packed light brown sugar
¾ cup light corn syrup
¼ cup water
20 miniature marshmallows
½ cup peanut butter
¼ cup butter or margarine
½ cup undiluted evaporated milk
1 teaspoon vanilla extract

1. Combine the brown sugar, corn syrup, and water in a small heavy saucepan. Stir over low heat until sugar is dissolved.
2. Increase heat and bring mixture to boiling. Wash down crystals from sides of pan with a pastry brush dipped in warm water.
3. Set candy thermometer in place. Cook, stirring occasionally to prevent scorching, until thermometer registers 234°F (soft ball stage), washing down crystals from sides of pan with a pastry brush dipped in fresh water each time.
4. Remove from heat and stir in remaining ingredients. Stir until smooth and creamy.
5. Serve warm as a topping for ice cream. Remaining sauce may be refrigerated; reheat before serving.

About 2 cups sauce

Sea-Foam Sauce

½ cup firmly packed brown sugar
¼ cup sugar
6 tablespoons water
1½ teaspoons light corn syrup
½ teaspoon cider vinegar
⅛ teaspoon salt
1 egg white
½ cup chilled whipping cream, whipped

1. Combine in a saucepan the sugars, water, corn syrup, vinegar, and salt. Stir over low heat until sugars are dissolved. Increase heat and bring mixture rapidly to boiling. Cover saucepan and boil mixture gently 5 minutes.
2. Uncover saucepan and set a candy thermometer in place. Continue cooking without stirring. During cooking, wash down crystals from sides of saucepan with a pastry brush dipped in water. Cook until thermometer registers 230°F (thread stage). Remove from heat.
3. Beat egg white until stiff, not dry, peaks are formed. Continue beating egg white while pouring the hot syrup over it in a thin steady stream (do not scrape bottom and sides of pan). Fold in whipped cream.
4. Serve over steamed pudding.

About 3 cups sauce

Apricot Sauce

1½ cups apricot jam
½ cup water
2 tablespoons sugar
1 tablespoon apricot brandy

1. Combine jam, water, and sugar in a saucepan. Bring to boiling and cook over low heat 5 to 10 minutes, stirring to prevent scorching.
2. Force mixture through a sieve. Stir in apricot brandy. Serve hot or cold.

About 1¾ cups sauce

Banana Fluff

3 ripe bananas, mashed
Dash salt
1½ teaspoons lemon juice
⅓ cup whipping cream
1 cup confectioners' sugar

1. Combine bananas, salt, and lemon juice. Beat in cream, using a rotary beater, adding sugar gradually.
2. Serve as topping for gingerbread.

2⅔ cups sauce

Elegant Purple Plum Sauce

½ cup sugar
⅓ cup light corn syrup
⅔ cup water
12 fresh purple plums, rinsed, pitted, and quartered
1 tablespoon cold water
1 tablespoon cornstarch
1 teaspoon grated lemon peel
8 whole cloves
1 teaspoon lemon juice
½ teaspoon vanilla extract

1. Combine the sugar, corn syrup, and the ⅔ cup water in a saucepan. Place over medium heat and stir until sugar is dissolved. Bring to boiling. Add plums; reduce heat and simmer, uncovered, until fruit is tender but not mushy. Remove plums from syrup and set aside.
2. Stir 1 tablespoon cold water into cornstarch to form a smooth paste. Gradually add cornstarch mixture to the hot syrup, stirring constantly.
3. Add lemon peel and cloves to sauce. Bring rapidly to boiling, stirring constantly. Cook until mixture is thick and clear. Return plums to sauce and heat thoroughly.
4. Remove from heat and blend in lemon juice and vanilla extract. Remove cloves. Serve sauce hot or cold with ice cream or over cake slices.

About 1¾ cups sauce

Note: If desired, fold 1 cup chilled whipping cream, whipped, into cooled sauce.

Fresh Raspberry Sauce

2 cups fresh raspberries, rinsed,
   hulled, and thoroughly drained
½ cup sugar
1 tablespoon cold water
1½ teaspoons cornstarch

1. Force raspberries through a sieve into a small heavy saucepan; discard seeds. Blend in sugar.
2. Stir water into cornstarch to make a smooth paste. Thoroughly blend with berry mixture.
3. Stirring gently and constantly, bring rapidly to boiling. Continue to stir and boil about 3 minutes. Set aside to cool. Chill thoroughly.

About 1 cup sauce

Note: For Strawberry Sauce, use rinsed and hulled **strawberries.**

Rosy Ginger Sauce

1 pound fresh rhubarb
1 pint fresh strawberries
½ cup sugar
2 teaspoons cornstarch
½ teaspoon ground allspice
½ cup sugar
2 tablespoons finely chopped
   preserved ginger

1. Cut rhubarb into ¾-inch slices (do not peel, if tender). Rinse, hull, and slice strawberries.
2. Combine rhubarb and ½ cup sugar in a heavy saucepan; cover tightly and cook until rhubarb is tender (about 5 minutes).
3. Meanwhile, mix together the cornstarch, allspice, and ½ cup sugar. Stirring constantly, gradually add to rhubarb and cook until mixture boils and thickens slightly.
4. Add strawberries and ginger. Cook 2 to 3 minutes, stirring occasionally. Cool before serving over sponge cake or ice cream.

About 3 cups sauce

Raspberry Sauce

2 packages (10 ounces each) frozen
   raspberries, thawed (do not
   drain)
¼ cup sugar
2 tablespoons light brown sugar
2 teaspoons cornstarch
   Few grains salt
½ teaspoon lime juice
¼ teaspoon grated lime peel

1. Force raspberries through a sieve into a saucepan; discard seeds. Combine the sugars, cornstarch, and salt; stir into raspberries.
2. Bring rapidly to boiling, stirring constantly; boil about 3 minutes. Remove from heat and stir in lime juice and peel. Set aside to cool. Chill thoroughly.

About 1⅓ cups sauce

Sweetened Whipped Cream

1 cup chilled whipping cream
3 tablespoons confectioners' sugar
1 teaspoon vanilla extract

1. Using a chilled bowl and chilled beater, beat whipping cream until it stands in soft peaks. With final few strokes, beat in confectioners' sugar and vanilla extract until blended.
2. Set in refrigerator if not used immediately. If whipped cream is not stiff enough when ready to use, beat again.

About 2 cups whipped cream

Cointreau Whipped Cream: Follow recipe for Sweetened Whipped Cream. Decrease sugar to 4 teaspoons and substitute **2 tablespoons Cointreau** for the vanilla extract.

Cocoa Whipped Cream: Follow recipe for Sweetened Whipped Cream. Omit sugar and add ¼ **cup instant cocoa** mix during last few strokes.

Strawberry Sauce

2 cups water
1 cup sugar
  Few grains salt
4 teaspoons lemon juice
1 tablespoon orange juice
1 quart strawberries, washed and
  hulled

1. Combine water, sugar, and salt in a heavy saucepan. Stir in lemon and orange juices. Bring rapidly to boiling, stirring constantly until sugar is dissolved.
2. Skim off foam and boil 5 minutes. Add strawberries and boil 1 minute longer.
3. Cool and chill. Serve over thick slices of pound or angel food cake.

About 1 quart sauce

Note: If desired, omit orange juice and substitute 1 teaspoon vanilla extract. Add to sauce before chilling.

Luscious Butterscotch Sauce

1 cup firmly packed light brown
  sugar
⅓ cup butter
⅓ cup cream or half-and-half
  Few grains salt

1. Combine all ingredients in a small heavy saucepan; stir over low heat until sugar is dissolved.
2. Increase heat to medium and bring mixture to boiling, stirring occasionally. Boil 5 minutes without stirring. Serve warm.

About 1¼ cups sauce

Index